高职高专经济管理类创新教材

实用会计英语
（第2版）

龚玲玲　主　编
鲍晓敏　副主编

清华大学出版社
北　京

内 容 简 介

本书以作者编著的面向在华外企财务人员的岗前培训讲义为蓝本，针对会计专业英语的核心目标，精炼了会计实务中所必需的会计专业英语知识与技能。本书选用单词巧记、情景模拟、口语对话、句型翻译、角色扮演、案例分析、综合模拟项目训练等丰富的方法，通过阐述会计英语在服务业、商业和制造业三大行业的应用，达到预期的知识传达与能力训练的目标。本书还科学地融入了英国、美国、加拿大、澳大利亚等国家/地区在国际会计领域较具影响力的会计执业资格考试的内容，很适合作为入门教材为会计人员参加 ACCA、AICPA 等考试打基础，并为计划去海外学习财会类专业的人员提供知识储备。在这一版中，我们还融入了党的二十大精神，并特别关注了数字化对会计行业的影响。

本书适合作为涉外会计、国际经济与贸易、国际工商管理等专业的高职、高专及成人高等院校学生的教材或教学参考书，也可作为外企财务人员从事英语会计工作的培训教材或参考用书。

本书封面贴有清华大学出版社防伪标签，无标签者不得销售。

版权所有，侵权必究。举报：010-62782989，beiqinquan@tup.tsinghua.edu.cn。

图书在版编目(CIP)数据

实用会计英语/龚玲玲主编. —2 版. —北京：清华大学出版社，2024.2
高职高专经济管理类创新教材
ISBN 978-7-302-65277-9

Ⅰ.①实⋯ Ⅱ.①龚⋯ Ⅲ.①会计－英语－高等职业教育－教材 Ⅳ.①F23

中国国家版本馆 CIP 数据核字(2024)第 034711 号

责任编辑：刘远菁
封面设计：常雪影
版式设计：方加青
责任校对：马遥遥
责任印制：杨　艳

出版发行：清华大学出版社
网　　址：https://www.tup.com.cn，https://www.wqxuetang.com
地　　址：北京清华大学学研大厦 A 座　　邮　编：100084
社 总 机：010-83470000　　邮　购：010-62786544
投稿与读者服务：010-62776969，c-service@tup.tsinghua.edu.cn
质量反馈：010-62772015，zhiliang@tup.tsinghua.edu.cn

印 装 者：三河市铭诚印务有限公司
经　　销：全国新华书店
开　　本：185mm×260mm　　印　张：11.75　　字　数：217 千字
版　　次：2014 年 5 月第 1 版　2024 年 2 月第 2 版　印　次：2024 年 2 月第 1 次印刷
定　　价：49.00 元

产品编号：101635-01

本书在第一版的基础上进行了全面更新和扩充,新增了"财务报表分析""数字化世界中的会计"两个单元,旨在为学习者提供与会计领域相关的最新英语学习材料,帮助读者提升在会计领域的英语能力,使读者无论是在学术研究、职业发展,还是在国际交流方面,都能如鱼得水。

在这一版中,我们融入了党的二十大精神,将党的二十大报告中与会计相关的内容融入各单元的"Guidance 学习指导"模块,从而为学生传递党的最新理论成果。此外,我们还特别关注了数字化对会计行业的影响。数字化技术的迅猛发展已经改变了会计的工作方式和需求。因此,我们新增了"数字化世界中的会计"这个单元,讨论了与人工智能、大数据、云计算和流程自动化相关的会计知识。通过学习这部分内容,您将了解会计领域中最新的技术趋势和应用,以及数字化转型对会计职业的影响。

我们希望本书能够成为您学习会计英语的有力工具。无论您是会计专业的学生、从业人员,还是对会计领域感兴趣的人士,我们相信本书将为您提供宝贵的学习资源,请与我们一起踏上会计英语的学习之旅,开启更广阔的职业和学术发展前景吧!

本书是校企合作、工学结合的成果。本书以作者编著的面向在华外企财务人员的岗前培训讲义为蓝本,经过多次调整,涵盖了会计实务中所必需的会计专业英语知识与技能,详细地解答了初次接触国外会计的人员在学习与工作中的常见困惑,可以作为会计人员从事英语会计工作的参考书。本书还科学地融入了英国、美国、加拿大、澳大利亚等国家/地区在国际会计领域较具影响力的会计执业资格考试的内容,适合作为会计人员参加ACCA(英国特许公认会计师公会)、AICPA(美国注册会计师协会)等考试的入门教材,为去海外学习财会类专业的人员提供知识储备。本书在编写过程中,充分发挥"浅、宽、精、用"的教学改革思想,精心编排,充分体现应用型职业技术教育模式的特色与教育对象的特点,在编写思路、载体选取和案例编写等方面有很强的独创性。

本书作者从事会计专业英语教学、外企职员财会英语培训及ACCA考前培训十余年,也曾在外企担任财务主管,拥有财会专业海外求学与教学经历,不仅熟悉中外会计专业知识,还具备丰富的会计英语教学与实践经验。此外，著名跨国财会业务流程外包企业简柏特(大连)有限公司财务运行中心副总裁何大玉女士，职业教育经验丰富的澳大利亚本迪哥职业技术学院(Bendigo TAFE)教师安妮·M·琼斯(Anne M. Jones)女士，新西兰会计师协会委员、澳大利亚莫纳什大学(Monash University)财务会计教授朵·科奇兰(Dot Cochran)博士为本书的前期开发提供了支持与指导。特别感谢ACCA官方认证黄金级培训机构中博诚通国际、大连新财经培训学校的ACCA讲师们，他们分享了多年积累的培训经验，参与了本书的编写工作。在海外会计师事务所有十余年从业经验的贵荣广讲师，大连职业技术学院外语教学部的关宜讲师，工商管理学院的张瑜、于威讲师也参与了本书的编写工作，关宜讲师完成全书的校对工作。衷心感谢诸位为本书的创作贡献智慧和付出努力！

受专业视野和写作水平限制，书中难免存在不足之处，恳请读者不吝指正，我们将认真修订和完善。反馈邮箱：wkservice@vip.163.com。

为更好地服务读者，本书提供参考译文和答案，并附赠配套电子课件，读者扫描下方二维码即可下载。

作者

2023年6月

UNIT 1	THE WORLD OF ACCOUNTING	1
LESSON 1	ACCOUNTING AND ITS ENVIRONMENT	2
LESSON 2	ACCOUNTING CONCEPTUAL FRAMEWORK	11
LESSON 3	ACCOUNTING ELEMENTS, EQUATION, AND DOUBLE ENTRY BOOKKEEPING	19
LESSON 4	ACCOUNTING CYCLE	25
PROJECT 1		39

UNIT 2	ACCOUNTING FOR SERVICE BUSINESS	41
LESSON 1	SERVICE BUSINESS AND ITS ACCOUNTING CYCLE	42
LESSON 2	RECORD TRANSACTIONS FOR SERVICE BUSINESS	47
PROJECT 2		58

UNIT 3	ACCOUNTING FOR MERCHANDISING BUSINESS	70
LESSON 1	MERCHANDISING BUSINESS AND ITS OPERATING CYCLE	71
LESSON 2	RECORD PURCHASE TRANSACTIONS FOR MERCHANDISING BUSINESS	75
LESSON 3	RECORD SALES TRANSACTIONS FOR MERCHANDISING BUSINESS	81
PROJECT 3		86

UNIT 4	ACCOUNTING FOR MANUFACTURING BUSINESS	92
LESSON 1	MANUFACTURING BUSINESS AND ITS OPERATING CYCLE	93
LESSON 2	ANALYZE THE "COST OF GOODS MANUFACTURED"	100
LESSON 3	RECORD TRANSACTIONS FOR MANUFACTURING BUSINESS	106
PROJECT 4		112

UNIT 5	FINANCIAL STATEMENTS	114
LESSON 1	AN OVERVIEW OF FINANCIAL STATEMENTS	115
LESSON 2	BALANCE SHEET	118

LESSON 3	INCOME STATEMENT	125
LESSON 4	CASH FLOW STATEMENT	130
PROJECT 5		136

UNIT 6 INTERPRETATION OF FINANCIAL STATEMENTS ... 139

| LESSON 1 | INTRODUCTION TO FINANCIAL STATEMENT INTERPRETATION | 140 |
| LESSON 2 | FINANCIAL RATIO ANALYSIS | 146 |

UNIT 7 ACCOUNTING IN A DIGITAL WORLD ... 158

| LESSON 1 | THE DIGITAL WORLD AND BUSINESS ENVIRONMENT | 159 |
| LESSON 2 | TECHNOLOGIES IN A DIGITAL WORLD | 166 |

APPENDIX ... 178
REFERENCES ... 180

UNIT 1
THE WORLD OF ACCOUNTING

您好！
　　我是Aston会计公司培训部的Helen。我主要负责新员工的会计基础知识培训，请您跟着我们的新员工一起来学习吧！

Goals 学习目标

- Have general knowledge of accounting and its environment, including types of business and the role of accounting in the business, users and their specific needs of accounting information, accounting profession, professional accounting bodies, and accounting regulatory system.
- Get familiar with accounting conceptual framework.
- Get familiar with accounting elements and the accounting equation.
- Master the skills of double entry bookkeeping.

Guidance 学习指导

　　人们管理经济、追求经济效益的进程推动了会计的产生与发展。生产力的不断发展、管理水平的提高及人类对经济效益的更高追求，会相应地对会计提出新的要求。党的二十大报告强调"实行更加积极主动的开放战略"，但由于各国的生产技术、生产关系、经济体制和上层建筑等不同，各国的会计也有所差异。随着国际筹资、投资活动与跨国经营活动的增加，在会计方面，为尽可能地消除各国之间的差异，会计处理正趋向某种程度的国际协调，即要求会计成为"国际商业语言"。

ACCOUNTING AND ITS ENVIRONMENT

GOALS 学习目标

- Have general knowledge of different types of business and the role of accounting in the business.
- Have general knowledge of the users of accounting information and their specific information needs.
- Have general knowledge of accounting profession, important professional accounting bodies, and accounting regulatory system.

MODULE 1 学以致用

Look at the pictures and match them with the correct words in the box.

customer	supplier	lender	government	competitor
investor	the public	employee	management	labor union
manufacturing	merchandising	service		

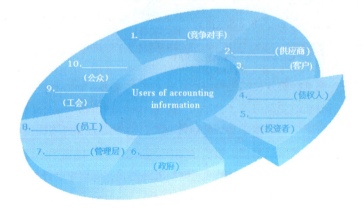

11. (服务业)_____   12. (制造业)_____   13. (商业)_____

MODULE 2 手不释卷

A. Read the following information about accounting and its environment.

1. Nature of Business

1) Types of Business Entity

A business can be organized in three different ways: manufacturing, merchandising, and service business, as shown in Exhibit 1-1.

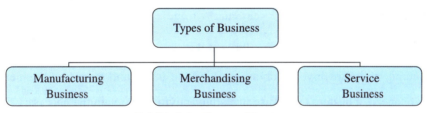

Exhibit 1-1　Types of Business

A manufacturing business converts materials into finished products through the use of machinery and labor.

A merchandising business must first purchase merchandises from other businesses (such as manufacturers or distributors) and then sell them to customers.

A service business provides services rather than products to customers.

2) Forms of Business

Three different forms of business are proprietorship (or sole trader), partnership, and corporation, as shown in Exhibit 1-2.

A proprietorship is owned and managed by one person, although there might be any number of employees. A proprietorship is fully and personally liable for any losses that the business might make.

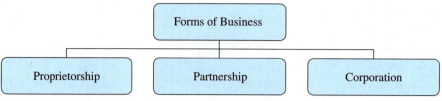

Exhibit 1-2　Forms of Business

A partnership is a business owned jointly by a number of partners. The partners are jointly liable for any losses that the business might make.

A corporation is owned by shareholders. Most corporations are limited liability corporations. For a limited liability corporation, the shareholders will not be personally liable for any losses the corporation incurs. The liability is limited to the nominal value of the shares they own. This limited liability is achieved by treating the corporation as a completely separate legal entity.

3) Types of Business Activities

Three different types of business activities are financing activities, investing activities, and operating activities, as shown in Exhibit 1-3.

Exhibit 1-3　Types of Business Activities

Financing activities involve obtaining funds to begin and operate a business. After funds are financed, a business must use investing activities to obtain the necessary resources to start and operate the business. Once resources have been acquired, a business uses the resources to implement its operating activities.

2. Objectives of Accounting (Shown in Exhibit 1-4)

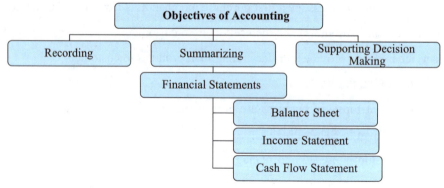

Exhibit 1-4　Objectives of Accounting

The objectives of accounting are shown in Exhibit 1-4: recording the business transactions; summarizing the business transactions within a period in order to provide information about the company in the forms of financial statements, such as balance sheet, income statement, cash flow statement, etc. (see Exhibit 1-5 which briefly shows the information in each of the financial statements); supporting decision making.

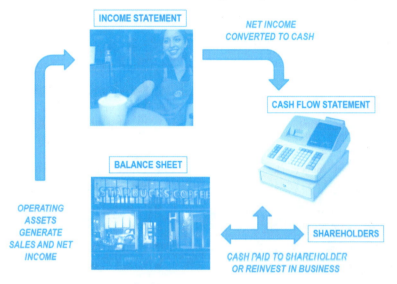

Exhibit 1-5   Summary of Information in the Financial Statements

3. Users of Accounting Information (Shown in Exhibit 1-6)

In general, users of accounting information are divided into two major categories: internal information users and external information users.

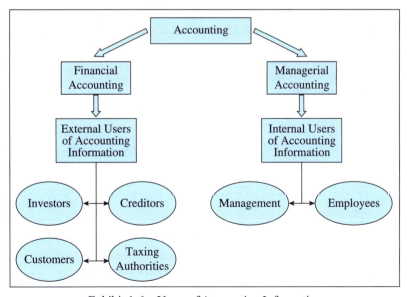

Exhibit 1-6   Users of Accounting Information

As is illustrated in Exhibit 1-6, financial accounting is concerned with the production of financial statements for external users. Management (or managerial) accounting provides much more detailed and up-to-date information for the management.

4. Types of Accounting (Shown in Exhibit 1-7)

Types of Accounting

Financial Accounting

- Produce summary financial statements for external users.
- Prepared annually (every six months or quarterly in some countries).
- Normally required by law.
- Show past performance and current position.
- Information provided in accordance with accounting standards.

Management Accounting

- Produce detailed accounts used by the management.
- Prepared monthly, often on a rolling basis.
- Not mandatory.
- Include budgets and forecasts of future activities and reflect past performance.
- Information provided in accordance with the requirement of management.

Exhibit 1-7   Types of Accounting

5. Accounting Regulatory System (Shown in Exhibit 1-8)

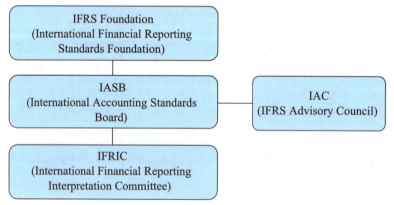

Exhibit 1-8   Accounting Regulatory System

The IFRS Foundation is the supervisory body for the IASB.

IASB is responsible for adopting existed International Accounting Standards (IAS), developing and issuing new accounting standards called International Financial Reporting Standards (IFRS). The logo of IASB is shown in Exhibit 1-9.

Exhibit 1-9　Logo of IASB

The IFRIC issues rapid guidance on accounting matters where divergent interpretations of IFRS have arisen.

IAC provides a forum for the IASB to consult a wider range of interested parties affected by the IASB's work.

6. Professional Accounting Bodies

专业会计团体	使用地区	缩写
Association of International Accountants	International	AIA
American Institute of Certified Public Accountants	U.S.	AICPA
Association of Chartered Certified Accountants	U.K.	ACCA

B. Learn the new words and phrases in the above passage and try to make sentences with them.

New Words

proprietorship	[prə'praiətəʃip]	n. 独资经营
partnership	['pɑːtnəʃip]	n. 合作关系，合伙企业
financing	[fai'nænsiŋ]	n. 筹集资金，融资
investing	[in'vestiŋ]	n. 投资
operating	['ɔpəreitiŋ]	n. 经营
communicate	[kə'mjuːnikeit]	vt. 沟通，交流
summarize	['sʌməraiz]	vt. 总结，概括
investor	[in'vestə]	n. 投资者
creditor	['kreditə]	n. 债权人，债主
globalization	[ˌgləubəlai'zeiʃn]	n. 全球化
standard	['stændəd]	n. 准则，标准

Useful Expressions and Knowledge

1. General Motors 美国通用汽车公司
2. financial statement 财务报表
3. decision maker 决策者
4. balance sheet 资产负债表
5. income statement 利润表
6. cash flow statement 现金流量表
7. government agencies 政府部门
8. managerial accounting 管理会计
9. tax bureau 税务局
10. financial accounting 财务会计
11. ACCA (英国)特许公认会计师公会

ACCA成立于1904年,是目前世界上最大及最有影响力的专业会计师组织之一,也是在运作上通向国际化及发展最快的会计师专业团体。

12. IASB 国际会计准则理事会

IASB(International Accounting Standards Board,国际会计准则理事会),前身是IASC(International Accounting Standards Committee,国际会计准则委员会),于2000年全面重组,主要负责制定和发布国际会计准则,促进国际会计的协调。

C. Test your understanding.

1. The "Big Four" are the four largest international accountancy firms. Please write their Chinese names in the blanks.

(1)_____ (2)_____ (3)_____ (4)_____

2. Match the words listed in the left box with the correct explanations in the right box.

A. Manufacturing business
B. Sole trader
C. Proprietorship
D. Merchandising business
E. Partnership
F. Service business
G. Corporation

(1) A business providing services rather than products to customers.
(2) A business which sells products to customers, but should first convert materials into finished products through the use of machinery and labor.
(3) A business owned and operated by one person.
(4) A business owned and operated by two or more people.
(5) A business organized as a separate legal entity.
(6) A business purchasing merchandises from other businesses and selling them to customers.

3. Fill in the blanks with correct words.

(1) _____(投资者) are interested in their potential profits and the security of their investments.

(2) _____(管理层) need detailed and up-to-date information such as profitability of individual departments and products, in order to control their business and plan for the future.

(3) _____(员工) need to know if an employer can offer secure employment and salaries.

(4) _____(债权人) need to know if they will be repaid, which will depend on the solvency of the company.

(5) _____(供应商) need to know the financial health of a business before agreeing to supply goods.

(6) _____(顾客) need to know if a company can continue to supply them in the future.

(7) _____(竞争对于) wish to compare their own performance with that of other companies and learn about their rivals.

(8) _____(政府) needs to use accounting information to figure a company's tax liabilities and watch over the company's adherence on regulations.

MODULE 3 博学多才

A. Visit the relevant website and write down some useful information you've learnt from it in English.

https://www.accaglobal.com/

推荐理由：英国特许公认会计师公会的官方网站，提供丰富的信息，包括ACCA考试资料、会计职业培训与发展资讯，以及会计专业前沿研究报告等。

_____

_____

B. Help your understanding.

"四大"会计师事务所

◆ KPMG(毕马威)

KPMG专门提供审计、税务和咨询等服务，业务遍及全球。在全球143个国家/地区，拥有员工约265 000名。主要客户包括美国通用电气、壳牌公司、辉瑞制药、雀巢公司、奔驰公司、百事可乐、花旗银行等。

◆ Ernst & Young(安永)

Ernst & Young专门提供审计与鉴证、税务咨询与筹划、财务咨询等服务。已有百年历史，业务遍及150个国家/地区，拥有员工约248 000名。主要客户包括英特尔、可口可乐、沃尔玛、麦当劳等。

◆ PwC(普华永道)

PwC专门提供审计、税务、人力资源、交易、危机管理等服务。业务遍及154个国家/地区，拥有员工约161 000名。主要客户包括埃克森、IBM、强生公司、戴尔电脑、福特汽车、雪佛兰、诺基亚等。

◆ Deloitte(德勤)

Deloitte专门提供审计、企业管理咨询、财务咨询、风险管理及税务等服务。业务遍及150个国家/地区，拥有员工约345 000名。主要客户包括微软公司、宝洁、美国通用汽车公司等。

LESSON 2
ACCOUNTING CONCEPTUAL FRAMEWORK

GOALS 学习目标

- Get familiar with accounting conceptual framework.
- Be able to explain underlying assumptions, principles, and constraints of accounting information.

MODULE 1 学以致用

Fill in the blanks with proper currency names and codes.

例：1. 货币名称：美元
　　　英文名称：U.S. Dollar
　　　货币代码：USD

2. 货币名称：_____
　　英文名称：_____
　　货币代码：_____

3. 货币名称：_____
　　英文名称：_____
　　货币代码：_____

4. 货币名称：_____
　　英文名称：_____
　　货币代码：_____

5. 货币名称：_____
   英文名称：_____
   货币代码：_____

6. 货币名称：_____
   英文名称：_____
   货币代码：_____

7. 货币名称：_____
   英文名称：_____
   货币代码：_____

8. 货币名称：_____
   英文名称：_____
   货币代码：_____

MODULE 2 手不释卷

A. Read the following information about accounting conceptual framework.

The accounting conceptual framework normally includes four basic assumptions, four basic principles, four basic constraints, and four qualitative characteristics of financial information.

1. Basic Accounting Assumptions (Shown in Exhibit 1-10)

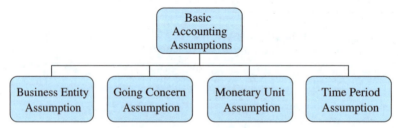

Exhibit 1-10　Basic Accounting Assumptions

- ◆ Business entity assumption: the business functions as a legal or financial entity separate from its owners or any other businesses.
- ◆ Going concern assumption: the business will operate for the foreseeable future

without significantly curtailing its activities.

◇ Monetary unit assumption: all the amounts listed in the financial statements use one stable currency.

◇ Time period assumption: all the transactions reported did in fact occur within the time period as listed.

2. Basic Accounting Principles (Shown in Exhibit 1-11)

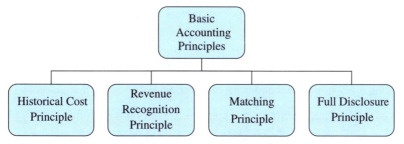

Exhibit 1-11　Basic Accounting Principles

◇ Historical cost principle: assets are recorded as the amount of cash or cash equivalents paid or fair value of the consideration given for them.

◇ Two revenue recognition principles: accrual basis accounting and cash basis accounting.

- Under accrual basis accounting, revenues are recognized as soon as a product has been sold or a service has been performed, regardless of when the money is actually received.
- Under cash basis accounting, revenues are recognized when cash is received.

◇ Matching principle: expenses in the financial statements must be matched with the revenue. The value of the expense is included in the financial statements when the product is sold, not necessarily when the invoice is issued.

◇ Full disclosure principle: the information pertinent to make a reasonable judgment on the company's finances must be included, as long as the costs to obtain the information is reasonable.

3. Basic Accounting Constraints (Shown in Exhibit 1-12)

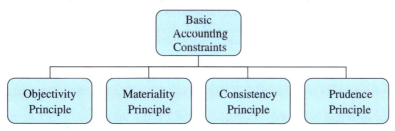

Exhibit 1-12　Basic Accounting Constraints

- Objectivity principle: all the information included in the financial statements must be supported by independent, verifiable evidence.
- Materiality principle: if a piece of information could influence users' decisions, it is material or significant. The financial statements must include information that is significant to a reasonable third party.
- Consistency principle: the company is required to use the same accounting methods and principles each year and any variation must be reported in the financial statement notes.
- Prudence principle: the company is required to include a degree of caution when making estimates under conditions of uncertainty. It ensures that assets and incomes are not overstated and liabilities or expenses are not understated.

4. Qualitative Characteristics of Financial Statements (Shown in Exhibit 1-13)

- Relevance principle: assisting users in evaluating financial performance; being helpful in predicting future performance; being helpful in confirming past prediction.
- Reliability principle: faithful representation; free from material error; substance over form; neutrality; prudence; completeness.
- Comparability principle: being able to compare with other businesses; being able to compare with previous periods' results.
- Understandability principle: enabling users to understand.

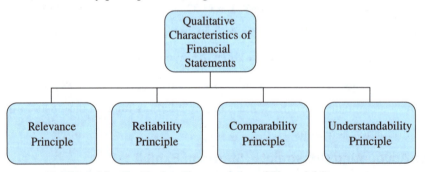

Exhibit 1-13　Qualitative Characteristics of Financial Statements

It is unlikely that all of the qualitative characteristics can be satisfied. There will be conflicts between them. Sometimes the information that is most relevant is not the most reliable or vice versa. As Exhibit 1-14 shows, an accountant must ensure the balance between relevance and reliability. In such a conflict, the information that is most relevant and that is reliable should be used.

Exhibit 1-14　Balance Between Relevance and Reliability

B. Learn the new words and phrases in the above passage and try to make sentences with them.

New Words

assumption	[əˈsʌmpʃn]	n. 假设
principle	[ˈprinsəpl]	n. 原则
constraint	[kənˈstreint]	n. 约束
qualitative	[ˈkwɔlitətiv]	adj. 定性的，质量的
characteristic	[ˌkæriktəˈristik]	n. 特点，特性
entity	[ˈentiti]	n. 实体，独立存在体
monetary	[ˈmʌnitəri]	adj. 货币的
periodicity	[ˌpiəriəˈdisiti]	n. 周期性
recognition	[ˌrekəgˈniʃn]	n. 确认
matching	[ˈmætʃiŋ]	adj. 配比
disclosure	[disˈkləuʒə]	n. 公开，披露

Useful Expressions and Knowledge

1. accounting conceptual framework 会计概念框架

   国际上通常简称为CF，包含会计目标、会计基本假设、会计对象；会计要素及会计信息质量特征；会计要素的确认、计量、记录与报告。

2. business entity assumption 会计主体假设

business entity assumption 如根据英文直译，应译为商业主体假设，但在我国，人们普遍称之为会计主体假设。

3. periodicity assumption 会计分期假设

会计期间分为年度(annual)、半年度(half-year)、季度(season)和月度(monthly)。各国/地区采用的会计年度不同：很多国家/地区采用日历年(calendar year)制(1月1日至12月31日)，包括中国、德国、芬兰等大部分国家/地区；有些国家/地区采用4月1日至次年3月31日制，包括英国、加拿大、印度、日本等国；澳大利亚、瑞典等国采用7月1日至次年6月30日制；美国、泰国等国则采用10月1日至次年9月30日制；等等。

4. monetary unit assumption 货币计量假设

在我国，企业的会计核算以人民币为记账本位币。业务收支以外币计价的企业，也可选择以某种外币作为记账本位币，但编制会计报表时应当将其折算为人民币。

5. accrual basis accounting 权责发生制

对于已经实现的收入和已经发生或应当负担的费用，不论款项是否收付，都应当被记为当期的收入和费用。我国企业在会计核算中实行权责发生制。

6. cash basis accounting 收付实现制

收付实现制以收到或支付现金作为确认收入和费用的依据。我国行政、事业单位(除经营业务采用权责发生制外)采用收付实现制。

7. full disclosure principle 充分披露原则

C. Test your understanding.

1. Fill in the blanks with the proper words and expressions given below, and change the form if necessary.

A. going concern	B. monetary unit	C. periodicity	D. business entity
E. materiality	F. consistency	G. prudence	H. objectivity
I. comparability	J. reliability	K. understandability	L. relevance

(1) _____(会计主体/经济主体) assumption assumes that the business is separate from its owners or other businesses.

(2) _____(持续经营) assumption assumes that the business will be in operation for the foreseeable future.

(3) _____(货币计量) assumption assumes a stable currency is going to be the unit of recording.

(4) _____(会计分期) assumption assumes that the economic activities of an enterprise can be divided into artificial time periods.

(5) _____(客观性) principle requires accounting entries in the accounting records and the data reported in the financial statements should be based on objective evidence.

(6) _____(重要性) principle requires that the financial statements must include information that is significant to a reasonable third party.

(7) _____(一致性) principle requires the business should employ the same accounting procedures during each period. By doing that, the information prepared could be compared from period to period.

(8) _____(谨慎性) principle requires inclusion of a degree of caution when making estimates under conditions of uncertainty. It ensures that assets and incomes are not overstated and liabilities or expenses are not understated.

2. Choose the correct answer.

(1) Which of the following assumptions is the basis upon which personal assets of the owner are excluded from the business balance sheet? (　　)

　　A. Going concern.　　B. Business entity.　　C. Objectivity.　　D. Historical Cost.

(2) The underlined word "Matching" in Page 13 refers to the matching of (　　).

　　A. cash inflows and outflows　　　　B. assets and liabilities

　　C. liabilities and owners' equity　　　D. revenues and expenses

(3) Which of the following forms of business organizations are legal entities separate from their owners under the law? (　　)

　　A. Sole proprietorships, partnerships, and corporations.

　　B. Sole proprietorships and corporations.

　　C. Partnerships and sole proprietorships.

　　D. Corporations.

(4) The measure used to account for assets is (　　).

　　A. resale value　　B. market value　　C. historical cost

　　D. either historical cost or market value, whichever is more realistic

(5) Revenues are recognized when earned, and expenses are recognized when incurred, regardless of the time when the money is received or paid. This is an application of (   ).

    A. cash basis accounting   B. the matching process

    C. accrual accounting   D. the cash flow principle

(6) Which of the following events would be given accounting recognition? (   )

    A. Hiring an employee.   B. Receiving an order from a customer.

    C. Paying a supplier for inventory.   D. Arranging a bank overdraft.

MODULE 3 博学多才

Visit the relevant websites and write down some useful information you've learnt from it in English.

1. https://wiki.mbalib.com/wiki/GAAP

    推荐理由：会计界普遍接受并有相当权威支持的公认会计原则的中文翻译，可用于指导和规范企业财务会计行为。

_____

_____

_____

2. https://www.fasab.gov/accepted.html

    推荐理由：美国联邦财务会计准则咨询委员会官方网站中有关GAAP的英文内容。

_____

_____

_____

LESSON 3
ACCOUNTING ELEMENTS, EQUATION, AND DOUBLE ENTRY BOOKKEEPING

GOALS 学习目标

- Get familiar with accounting elements and the accounting equation.
- Master the skills of double entry bookkeeping.

MODULE 1 学以致用

Fill in the blanks with the proper words and expressions given below, and change the form if necessary.

> liability   owners' equity   asset   revenue   profit   expense

1. _____(资产) is a resource controlled by an entity as a result of a past event from which it is probable that future economic benefits will flow.

2. _____(负债) is a present obligation arising from a past event, the settlement of which results in an outflow of resources embodying future economic benefits.

3. _____(所有者权益) is the residual interest in the net assets of an entity after having deducted all liabilities.

4. _____(收入) are increases in economic benefits arising from the enhancement of assets or reduction in liability that result in increases in equity other than those arising from contributions from equity participants.

5. _____(费用) are decreases in economic benefits in the form of depletion of assets or increase in liabilities that result in decreases in equity other than those arising from distribution to equity participants.

6. _____(利润) are revenues deducted by expenses if the result is positive. Losses are revenues deducted by expenses if the result is negative. The profits (or losses) are transferred to the _____(所有者权益) of the balance sheet.

MODULE 2 手不释卷

A. Read the following information about accounting elements, equation, and double entry bookkeeping.

1. Accounting Elements

Assets, liabilities, and owners' (or shareholders') equity are the accounting elements related to the financial condition in the balance sheet. Revenues, expenses, and profits (or losses) are the accounting elements related to the financial performance in the income statement.

2. Accounting Equation

$$Assets = Liabilities + Owners' Equity$$

The accounting equation is a simple expression of the fact that at any point in time the assets of the business will be equal to its liabilities plus the owners' equity of the business. Please refer to Exhibit 1-15 as an example.

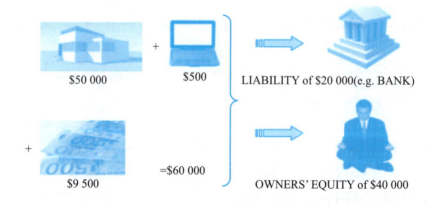

Exhibit 1-15 Example of Accounting Equation

Assets minus liabilities must be equal to owners' equity, also known as net assets.

$$Assets – Liabilities = Owners' Equity = Net Assets$$

The accounting equation can also be extended to include revenues and expenses of a business:

$$Assets = Liabilities + Owners' Equity + Profits (or Losses)$$

$$Assets = Liabilities + Owners' Equity + (Revenues － Expenses)$$

Every transaction that the business makes or enters into has two aspects to the accounting equation. This is known as duality concept.

3. Rule of Double Entry Bookkeeping (Shown in Exhibit 1-16)

Type of Ledger A/C	Nature of Ledger A/C	Increase	Decrease
REVENUE	CR	CR	DR
EXPENSE	DR	DR	CR
ASSET	DR	DR	CR
LIABILITY	CR	CR	DR
OWNERS EQUITY	CR	CR	DR

Exhibit 1-16   Rule of Double Entry Bookkeeping

The rule of double entry bookkeeping is that each business transaction must be recorded by an entry that has equal amount of debits (left side) and credits (right side).

As is illustrated in Exhibit 1-16, assets accounts are increased by debiting and decreased by crediting, and usually have debit balances, while liabilities and owners' equity accounts are increased by crediting and decreased by debiting, and usually have credit balances.

Example 1 Investing Capital

On Jan.1, 2022, Polo invested €10 000 in cash to start a retail business—Happy Shop which sells roses and chocolate.

Dual effects: Happy Shop had cash of €10 000; owners' equity increased by €10 000.

Dr: Cash on hand   €10 000   (assets ▲)

　　Cr: Capital   €10 000   (owners' equity ▲)

Example 2 Buying Inventory in Cash

On Jan. 3, 2022, Happy Shop bought 500 chocolate bars in cash and the cost of each bar was €5.

Dual effects: chocolate inventory increased by €2 500; cash decreased by €2 500.

Dr: Inventory   €2 500   (assets ▲)

　　Cr: Cash on hand   €2 500   (assets ▼)

Example 3 Buying Inventory on Credit

On Jan. 6, 2022, Happy Shop bought 200 red roses from Sunny Nursery and each rose cost €10.

Dual effects: Roses inventory increased by €2 000; current liability increased by €2 000.

Dr: Inventory €2 000 (assets ▲)

　　Cr: Accounts payable €2 000 (liabilities ▲)

B. Learn the new words and phrases in the above passage and try to make sentences with them.

New Words

shareholder	[ˈʃeə,həuldə]	n. 股东
equity	[ˈekwiti]	n. 权益
element	[ˈelimənt]	n. 要素
performance	[pəˈfɔːməns]	n. 业绩，工作成果
aspect	[ˈæspekt]	n. 方面
bookkeeping	[ˈbuk,kiːpiŋ]	n. 记账，簿记
debit	[ˈdebit]	n. 借方
credit	[ˈkredit]	n. 贷方
balance	[ˈbæləns]	n. 余额

Useful Expressions and Knowledge

1. accounting elements 会计要素
2. financial condition 财务状况
3. duality concept 复式原理
4. financial performance 财务业绩
5. accounting equation 会计等式
6. double entry bookkeeping 复式簿记

　　可将double entry bookkeeping 直译为复式簿记，国内常称之为借贷记账。

C. Test your understanding.

1. Analyze the following transactions and figure out how they will affect the accounting equation.

(1) Assets increase by $5 000 and liabilities increase by $3 000.

(2) Proprietorship falls by $3 000 and liabilities increase by $3 000.

(3) One asset increases by $14 000, other assets decrease by $7 000, and liabilities increase by $1 500.

(4) Assets increase by $2 350 and liabilities decrease by $1 560.

(5) A customer settled his account of $500 by cleaning his windows.

(6) The owner paid a business debt of $800 by drawing a cheque on his personal bank account.

2. Analyze the following transactions and figure out how the relevant accounting elements and journal entries will change.

(1) The owner contributed $1 000 to the business.

(2) Purchased a motor vehicle for $16 000 in cash.

(3) Purchased a motor vehicle on credit for $16 000.

(4) Received cash immediately for accounting fees.

(5) Sold goods on credit for $1 000 that originally cost $600.

(6) Paid creditors $100.

(7) Received $100 from debtors.

(8) The owner withdrew $100 for personal use.

(9) A debtor owing $1 000 has been declared bankruptcy and the trustee advises that no repayment is possible.

MODULE 3 博学多才

Help your understanding.

复式簿记的由来

复式簿记，最初叫意大利式借贷簿记法，是为了适应商人的需要而在意大利北部各城市自然发展起来的。目前保存下来的意大利最古老的会计账簿，是由德国史学家西夫金(Sieveking)发现的1211年佛罗伦萨银行家的簿记，现收藏于佛罗伦萨梅底棋·拉乌莱芝纳图书馆。在账簿中，按每个客户的姓名开立账户，用借贷上下连续的方式登记与顾客的各笔交易；各账户之间相互关联，可以进行转账。

  14世纪末到15世纪初是复式簿记的诞生阶段。1494年，意大利传教士卢卡·帕乔利(Luca Pacioli)出版了一部了不起的专著——《算术、几何、比例概要》(*Summade Arithmetica, Geometria, Proportioniet Proportionalita*)。该书共分五卷：第一卷论述代数和算术；第二卷论述商业算术和代数；第三卷论述簿记；第四卷论述货币和兑换；第五卷论述纯粹几何学和应用几何学。其中，关于借贷复式记账法的论述位于该书第三卷第九部第十一篇《计算与记录要论》。

LESSON 4
ACCOUNTING CYCLE

GOALS 学习目标

- Get familiar with the accounting cycle.
- Have general knowledge of the steps in the accounting cycle.
- Have general knowledge of the core concepts and relevant documents in the accounting cycle.

MODULE 1 学以致用

Fill in the blanks with the proper words and expressions given below, and change the form if necessary.

A. general journal　　B. source document　　C. worksheet
D. general ledger　　E. trial balance

1. A _____(原始凭证) may be a piece of contract, or a receipt, invoice, sales ticket, or cash register tape.

2. _____(普通日记账) is a book of original entry because it is where the first accounting record of a transaction is made from a source document.

3. _____(总账) is a book of accounts that contains a separate account for each account listed in the COA.

4. A _____(试算平衡表) is a list of all accounts showing the title and ending balance of the accounts.

5. The _____(工作表) lists all the accounts from the general ledger that has a balance or will have a balance after the adjusting entries are entered.

MODULE 2 手不释卷

A. Read the following information about the accounting cycle.

Exhibit 1-17 briefly shows the typical accounting steps involved in the accounting process. This is called the accounting cycle. The accounting cycle consists of the steps involved in accounting during a period of time.

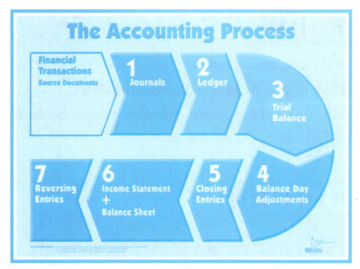

Exhibit 1-17   Typical Steps Involved in the Accounting Process

Step 1   Analyze source documents.

Each source document should be carefully studied to determine which accounts are affected. The examples of source documents are shown in Exhibit 1-18 below.

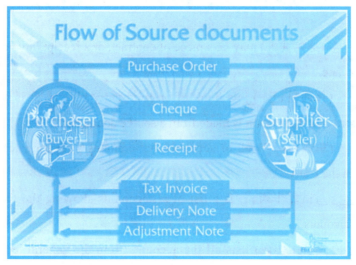

Exhibit 1-18   Examples of Source Documents

Step 2 Journalize the transactions in the general journal.

The debit followed by the credit of each transaction is recorded in the general journal by date and in chronological order. In addition, a brief explanation of the transaction is given. Please see the example of general journal in Exhibit 1-19.

	General Journal			Page 1	
	Date		Account Name and Description	Post Ref.	Debit ($)	Credit ($)	
1	2022						1
2	Oct.	1	Cash on hand	101	80 000		2
3			Capital—A. D. Brown	300		80 000	3
4			A. D. Brown invested cash to start business				4

Exhibit 1-19 Example of General Journal

Step 3 Post transactions from the general journal to the general ledger.

All amounts in the general journal are posted to the general ledger accounts. Such posting is done daily, weekly, or at regular time intervals. Please see the example of general ledger in Exhibit 1-20 and Exhibit 1-21.

Account Name: Cash on Hand					Account No.:101		
Date		Description	Post Ref.	Debit ($)	Credit ($)	Balance	
						Debit($)	Credit($)
2022							
Oct.	1	A. D. Brown invested cash to start business	GJ 1	80 000		80 000	

Exhibit 1-20 Example of General Ledger (1)

Account Name: Capital—A. D. Brown					Account No.:300		
Date		Description	Post Ref.	Debit ($)	Credit ($)	Balance	
						Debit($)	Credit($)
2022							
Oct.	1	A. D. Brown invested cash to start business	GJ 1		80 000		80 000

Exhibit 1-21 Example of General Ledger (2)

Step 4 Prepare a trial balance.

A trial balance is prepared in order to check the accuracy of the recording process by checking every debit entry made with an equal credit entry. Please see the trial balance statement in Exhibit 1-22.

Happy Shop
Trial Balance Statement as of Jan. 31, 2022 (€)

Account	Debit	Credit
Cash on hand	8 750	
Cash at bank	3 000	
Accounts receivable	2 000	
Inventory	500	
Fixed assets	1 000	
Accounts payable		500
Long-term loans		2 000
Capital		9 250
Sales revenue		8 000
Cost of sales	4 000	
Expenses	500	
Total	**19 750**	**19 750**

Exhibit 1-22 Example of Trial Balance Statement

Step 5 Prepare a worksheet, make adjustments, and complete the worksheet.

End-of-period worksheet (shown in Exhibit 1-23) is normally prepared to make ending period accounting steps easier. Under accrual basis accounting, we need to adjust some account balances at the end of each accounting period to achieve a proper matching of expenses (or costs) incurred with revenues earned.

There are four types of adjusting entries: apportioning recorded costs to periods benefited; apportioning recorded revenues to periods during which they are earned; accruing unrecorded expenses incurred; accruing unrecorded revenues earned.

Gymnasium and Health Club
Worksheet
as of Jun. 30, 2022 ($)

Account Title	(1) Unadjusted TB		(2) Adjustments		(3) Adjusted TB		(4) Income Statement		(5) Balance Sheet	
	DR	CR	DR	CR	DR	CR	DR	CR	DR	CR
Cash at bank	14 106				14 106				14 106	
Accounts receivable	24 805				24 805				24 805	
Prepaid insurance	(a) 2 894			(b)1 447	1 447				1 447	
Prepaid rent	3 526			588	2 938				2 938	
Stationery supplies	1 764			1 140	624				624	
Gym equipment	19 692				19 692				19 692	
Motor vehicle	(c)32 062				32 062				32 062	
Accounts payable		7 536				7 536				7 536
Bank loan		22 449				22 449				22 449
Capital		62 529				62 529				62 529
Drawing	941				941				941	
Gym fees revenue		4 984				4 984		4 984		
Squash fees revenue		7 519				7 519		7 519		
Membership fees revenue		4 839				4 839		4 839		
Staff wages expense	5 940		(f)424		6 364		6 364			
Equipment hiring expense	1 296				1 296		1 296			
Motor vehicle expense	276				276		276			
Advertising expense	2 025				2 025		2 025			
Sundry expense	529				529		529			
Subtotal	109 856	109 856								
Bank loan interest expense			150		150		150			
Interest payable				150		150				150
Accrued wages payable				(e)424		424				424
Motor vehicle accumulated depreciation				(d)561		561				561
Insurance expense			1 447		1 447		1 447			
Rent expense			588		588		588			
Depreciation expense			964		964		964			
Gym equipment accumulated depreciation				403		403				403
Stationery supplies expense			1 140		1 140		1 140			
Subtotal			4 713	4 713	111 394	111 394	14 779	17 342	96 615	94 052
Profit							2 563			2 563
Total							17 342	17 342	96 615	96 615

Exhibit 1-23   Example of End-of-period Worksheet

Step 6 Prepare financial statements using the worksheet as a guide.

The fourth pair of columns in the worksheet is income statement columns. Extend the amounts of revenues and expenses in the adjusted TB (adjusted trial balance) in the third pair of columns to the income statement columns, as shown in Exhibit 1-24.

Gymnasium and Health Club Monthly Income Statement as of Jun. 30, 2022 ($)	
Revenues	
Gym fees revenue	4 984
Squash fees revenue	7 519
Membership fees revenue	4 839
Total revenue	17 342
Expenses	
Staff wages expense	6 364
Equipment hiring expense	1 296
Motor vehicle expense	276
Advertising expense	2 025
Sundry expense	529
Bank loan interest expense	150
Insurance expense	1 447
Rent expense	588
Depreciation expense	964
Stationery supplies expense	1 140
Total expense	(14 779)
Net profit	2 563

Exhibit 1-24　Example of Income Statement

The fifth pair of columns in the worksheet is balance sheet columns. Extend the remaining amounts of accounts in the third pair of columns (other than revenues and expenses) to the balance sheet columns. The example of balance sheet is illustrated in Exhibit 1-25.

Gymnasium and Health Club Monthly Balance Sheet as of Jun. 30, 2022 ($)				
Assets		**Liabilities & Owners' equity**		
		Liabilities		
Current assets		*Current liabilities*		
Cash at bank	14 106	Accounts payable		7 536
Accounts receivable	24 805	Interests payable		150
Prepaid insurance	1 447	Wages payable		424
Prepaid rent	2 938	Total current liabilities		8 110
Stationery supplies	624	*Long-term liabilities*		
Total current assets	43 920	Bank loans		22 449
Non-current assets		Total long-term liabilities		22 449
Gym equipment	19 692	**Total liabilities**		**30 559**
Less: Accumulated depreciation	(403)	**Owners' Equity**		
Motor vehicle	32 062	Capital (Jun. 1)		62 529
Less: Accumulated depreciation	(561)	Add: Profit		2 563
Total non-current assets	50 790	Less: Drawings		(941)
		Capital (Jun. 30)		64 151
		Total owners' equity		**64 151**
Total assets	**94 710**	**Total liabilities and owners' equity**		**94 710**

Exhibit 1-25   Example of Balance Sheet

Step 7   Journalize and post the adjusting entries using the worksheet as a guide (as shown in Exhibit 1-26).

General Journal				Page 3
Date	Particulars	Post Ref.	DR($)	CR($)
Jun. 30	Bank loan interest expense	520	150	
	Interest payable	210		150
Jun. 30	Depreciation expense—motor vehicle	580	561	
	Motor vehicle accumulated depreciation	191		561
Jun. 30	Insurance expense	510	1 447	
	Prepaid insurance	110		1 447
Jun. 30	Rent expense	525	588	
	Prepaid rent	111		588
Jun. 30	Depreciation expense—gym equipment	580	403	
	Gym equipment accumulated depreciation	190		403
Jun. 30	Stationery supplies expense	530	1 140	
	Stationery supplies	120		1 140
Jun. 30	Staff wages expense	500	424	
	Accrued wages payable	245		424

Exhibit 1-26   Journalize Adjusting Entries in the General Journal

Step 8 Journalize and post the closing entries using the worksheet as a guide (as shown in Exhibit 1-27).

Date	General Journal Particulars	Page 1 DR($)	CR($)
Jun. 30	Gym fees revenue	4 984	
Jun. 30	Squash fees revenue	7 519	
Jun. 30	Membership fees revenue	4 839	
Jun. 30	Income summary		17 342
Jun. 30	Income summary	14 779	
Jun. 30	Staff wages expense		6 364
Jun. 30	Insurance expense		1 447
Jun. 30	Bank loan interest expense		150
Jun. 30	Rent expense		588
Jun. 30	Stationery supplies expense		1 140
Jun. 30	Equipment hiring expense		1 296
Jun. 30	Motor vehicle expense		276
Jun. 30	Advertising expense		2 025
Jun. 30	Sundry expense		529
Jun. 30	Gym equipment depreciation expense		403
Jun. 30	Motor vehicle depreciation expense		561
Jun. 30	Profit & Loss Summary	2 563	
Jun. 30	Capital		2 563

Exhibit 1-27　Journalize and Post the Closing Entries in the General Journal

B. Learn the new words and phrases in the above passage and try to make sentences with them.

New Words

account	[əˈkaunt]	n. 账，账户
journalizing	[ˈdʒəːnəlaiziŋ]	n. 日记账分录，流水分录
explanation	[ˌekspləˈneiʃn]	n. 解释，说明
ledger	[ˈledʒə]	n. 分类账
regular	[ˈregjulə]	adj. 定时的，定期的
prepare	[priˈpɛə]	vt. 准备，编制
adjust	[əˈdʒʌst]	vt. & vi. 调整
incur	[inˈkəː]	vt. 引起，产生(费用)
column	[ˈkɔləm]	n. 栏，纵列
apportion	[əˈpɔːʃn]	vt. 分配，分摊，摊销

> **Useful Expressions and Knowledge**
>
> 1. accounting cycle 会计循环
> 2. source document 原始凭证
> 3. general journal 普通日记账
> 4. general ledger 总账
> 5. trial balance 试算平衡
> 6. account balance 账户余额
> 7. balance sheet 资产负债表
> 8. financial statements 财务报表

C. Test your understanding.

Analyze the following transactions of Gymnasium and Health Club and try to make the adjusting entries as of Jun. 30, 2022.

Transaction 1 Apportioning recorded costs to periods benefited.

On Jun.1, 2022, Gymnasium and Health Club paid $2 894 for 2 months' general insurances by bank cheque (refer to (a) in Exhibit 1-23).

Transaction 2 Apportioning recorded revenues to periods during which they were earned.

On Jun.15, Gymnasium and Health Club received $500 from customer Andy for 2 months' massage service.

Transaction 3

On Jun. 30, about one quarter of service was completed.

Transaction 4 Accruing unrecorded expenses incurred.

Gymnasium and Health Club pays $1 485 for the staff's wages each week; the last wage of this period was paid on Jun. 29; at the end of this period, two days' (Jun. 29 and 30) services from the staff had not be paid.

Transaction 5 Accruing unrecorded revenues earned.

Gymnasium and Health Club provided training service to a local primary school for two weeks. The total amount to be received is $1 500.

MODULE 3 博学多才

Help your understanding.

1. 原始凭证 (source documents)

Analyze the source documents and try to record the transactions on the basis of the source documents.

◇ Sales Invoice

Direction: Please record the transaction into the general journal for Moorabbin Hardware on the basis of the sales invoice in Exhibit 1-28.

MOORABBIN HARDWARE 178 CHESTERTON ROAD MOORABBIN	TAX INVOICE NO. 782 3/5/2022
SOLD TO	Goss & Sons 78 Scott Street Beaumaris

YOUR ORDER NO. 414		TERMS	
QUANTITY	DESCRIPTION	UNIT PRICE($)	AMOUNT($)
2 tins	500 ml White Undercoat	13.00	26.00
1 tin	500 ml Chipboard White	14.50	14.50
1 bottle	Mineral Turps	2.00	2.00
1 unit	Medium Paint Brush	3.20	3.20
		Total	45.70

Exhibit 1-28　Sample Sales Invoice

Analysis: According to the sales invoice, Moorabbin Hardware should record the transaction as follows.

Dr: Accounts receivable　　$45.70
　　Cr: Sales revenue　　　　$45.70

◇ Credit Note

Direction: Please record the transaction in the general journal for Sleepy Bed Store on the basis of the credit note in Exhibit 1-29.

SLEEPY BED STORE........		CREDIT NOTE NO. B42	
200 MAIN STREET			
BEDWAY...............		2 / 3 / 2022	
CREDIT TO	Sleepy Ezy		
	124 Pillow Street, Snorerite		
INVOICE NO. *1012*		YOUR ORDER NO. *P132*	
REASON FOR CREDIT: *Damaged on delivery*			
QUANTITY	DESCRIPTION	UNIT PRICE($)	AMOUNT ($)
1	A348—Bedroom Suite	425.00	425.00
			425.00

Exhibit 1-29   Sample Credit Note

Analysis: According to the credit note, Sleepy Bed Store should record the transaction as follows.

Dr: Sales revenue $425

    Cr: Accounts receivable $425

◇ **Bank Cheque**

Direction: Please record the transaction in the general journal for John Smith on the basis of the bank cheque in Exhibit 1-30.

Exhibit 1-30   Sample Bank Cheque

Analysis: According to the bank cheque, John Smith should record the transaction as follows.

Dr: Expense (car repair expense) $100

    Cr: Cash at bank $100

2. 会计科目表 (chart of accounts)

会计科目表是针对特定目的而提供的会计整理表，附有账户名称与账号。为了便于编制会计凭证、登记账簿、查阅账目、实行会计电算化，为每个账户编一个固定的号码(简称科目编号)。Exhibit 1-31列出了部分常见的会计科目的中、英文形式。

编号	会计科目名称	Chart of Accounts
	一、资产类	Assets
1001	库存现金	cash on hand
1002	银行存款	cash at bank
1012	其他货币资金	other cash and cash equivalents
1031	存出保证金	refundable deposit
1101	交易性金融资产	tradable financial assets
1121	应收票据	notes receivable
1122	应收账款	accounts receivable
1123	预付账款	advanced payments
1131	应收股利	dividends receivable
1132	应收利息	interest receivable
1221	其他应收款	other receivables
1231	坏账准备	bad debt reserves
1303	贷款	loans
1304	贷款损失准备	loans depreciation reserves
1401	材料采购	supplies purchasing
1402	在途物资	supplies in transit
1403	原材料	raw materials
1404	材料成本差异	materials cost variance
1405	库存商品	finished goods
1406	发出商品	goods in delivery
1407	商品进销差价	difference between purchasing and selling prices
1408	委托加工物资	work in process—outsourced
1471	存货跌价准备	inventory falling price reserves
1511	长期股权投资	long-term investment on stock
1512	长期股权投资减值准备	stock rights investment depreciation reserves
1521	投资性房地产	property investment
1531	长期应收款	long-term accounts receivable
1541	存出资本保证金	refundable guaranteed deposit
1601	固定资产	fixed assets

Exhibit 1-31　Chart of Accounts

(续表)

编号	会计科目名称	Chart of Accounts
1602	累计折旧	accumulated depreciation
1603	固定资产减值准备	fixed assets depreciation reserves
1604	在建工程	construction-in-process
1605	工程物资	project goods and material
1606	固定资产清理	liquidation of fixed assets
1701	无形资产	intangible assets
1702	累计摊销	amortization
1703	无形资产减值准备	intangible assets depreciation reserves
1711	商誉	goodwill
1801	长期待摊费用	long-term deferred and prepaid expenses
1811	递延所得税资产	deferred income tax assets
1901	待处理财产损益	wait deal assets loss or income
	二、负债类	Liabilities
2001	短期借款	short-term borrowing
2002	存入保证金	promissory notes
2004	向中央银行借款	borrowing from central bank
2101	交易性金融负债	transactional financial liability
2201	应付票据	notes payable
2202	应付账款	accounts payable
2203	预收账款	deposit received
2211	应付职工薪酬	accrued wages (wages payable)
2221	应交税费	tax payable
2231	应付利息	interest payable
2232	应付股利	dividend payable
2241	其他应付款	other payables
2401	递延收益	deferral income
2501	长期借款	long-term loans
2502	应付债券	bonds payable
2701	长期应付款	long-term accounts payable
2901	递延所得税负债	deferral tax liabilities
	三、共同类	General
3001	清算资金往来	liquidity account
3002	货币兑换	currency exchange
3101	衍生工具	derivatives
3201	套期工具	terms

Exhibit 1-31　Chart of Accounts (Continued)

(续表)

编号	会计科目名称	Chart of Accounts
	四、所有者权益类	**Owners' Equity**
4001	实收资本	capital
4002	资本公积	capital reserves
4101	盈余公积	surplus reserves
4103	本年利润	current year profit/income summary
4104	利润分配	profit distribution
	五、成本类	**Costs**
5001	生产成本	manufactory costs
5101	制造费用	manufactory overheads
5201	劳务成本	labor costs
5301	研发支出	research and development costs
5401	工程施工	project in process
	六、损益类	**Incomes and Expenses**
6001	主营业务收入	prime operating revenue (core business revenue)
6011	利息收入	interest income
6021	手续费及佣金收入	transaction and commission income
6031	保费收入	insurance income
6041	租赁收入	rent income
6051	其他业务收入	other business revenues
6061	汇兑损益	foreign currency exchange profit or loss
6111	投资收益	investment income
6301	营业外收入	non-operating income
6401	主营业务成本	cost of goods sold
6402	其他业务成本	other business expenses
6411	利息支出	interest expense
6421	手续费及佣金支出	transaction and commission expense
6601	销售费用	sales expense
6602	管理费用	administrative expense
6603	财务费用	financial expense
6701	资产减值损失	asset depreciation expense
6711	营业外支出	non-operational expense
6801	所得税费用	income tax expense
6901	以前年度损益调整	profit or loss on adjustment

Exhibit 1-31　Chart of Accounts (Continued)

PROJECT 1

Background: Some typical transactions of different businesses which involve balance day adjustments are listed below.

Task: Please make the adjusting entries as of Jun. 30 and record them in the general journal for the businesses.

Transactions:

(1) Telephone expenses for Jun. amount to $300. This amount has not yet been recorded because it is not payable until Jul.

(2) On Apr. 1, the firm received $4 000 for the following four months' rent on surplus office space that they were letting out to a real estate agent. The amount received on Apr. 1 was recorded as liability.

(3) On Jun. 1, Construction Consultants invested $10 000 of surplus cash in a local bank. Interest, at the rate of 12 percent per annum, is payable at the end of every three months. The first receipt of interest is due on Sep. 1.

(4) The engineers receive a retainer of $500 per month from a State Highways Department. The retainer is paid on the last day of each month and is recorded as revenue on the day of receipt. However, the Highways Department has overlooked to make the payment due on Jun. 30.

(5) The Secretary's salary of $300 per week for the five days' work and the week ending on Wednesday, Jul. 3 will be paid on Jul. 3.

(6) On Feb. 1, the firm paid $2 400 of insurance premium for insurance cover for the next twelve months. The amount was recorded as an asset on Feb. 1.

(7) Depreciate office equipment, which cost $10 000 on Apr. 1 and has an expected useful life of 5 years with an expected scrap value of $2 000.

Direction and Relevant Table:

Prepare balance day adjusting entries, in general journal form (see Exhibit 1-32), for each of the above—the balance date is Jun. 30.

	Date	Account Name and Description	Post Ref.	Debit ($)	Credit ($)	
1						1
2						2
3						3
4						4
5						5
6						6

General Journal — Page 1

Exhibit 1-32　General Journal

UNIT 2

ACCOUNTING FOR SERVICE BUSINESS

您好!

我是艾德记账公司的会计John,我将在这几星期教我的新同事Mary为我们在伦敦的几个从事服务业的客户做会计核算。

同学们,跟着Mary一起学习"服务企业的会计核算"吧!

Goals 学习目标

- Have general knowledge of service businesses and the basic accounting cycle of service businesses.
- Master the skills of accounting for service businesses.

Guidance 学习指导

党的二十大报告指出:"构建优质高效的服务业新体系,推动现代服务业同先进制造业、现代农业深度融合。"随着经济的发展,世界服务产业占GDP的比重持续上升,在发展中国家约为60%,在发达国家高达70%。服务企业经营形式多样,行业分布广(包括交通运输、金融、旅游、广告、娱乐、电信、酒店、财会服务、软件与信息咨询等),很多企业是小规模纳税人,其在会计核算上也因其自身的行业特点而与其他企业有所不同。在会计英语中,由于服务企业不同于工商企业,会计人员在对服务企业进行会计核算时,不能拘泥于传统的模式。

LESSON 1
SERVICE BUSINESS AND ITS ACCOUNTING CYCLE

GOALS 学习目标

- Have general knowledge of service businesses and the basic accounting cycle of service businesses.
- Be able to name a few famous service businesses and get familiar with them.

MODULE 1 学以致用

Look at the pictures and match them with the correct words in the box.

entertainment	transportation	hospitality	obligation
telecommunications	accounting	financial	benefit
asset	equity	interest	resource

1. (娱乐)_____

2. (酒店服务)_____

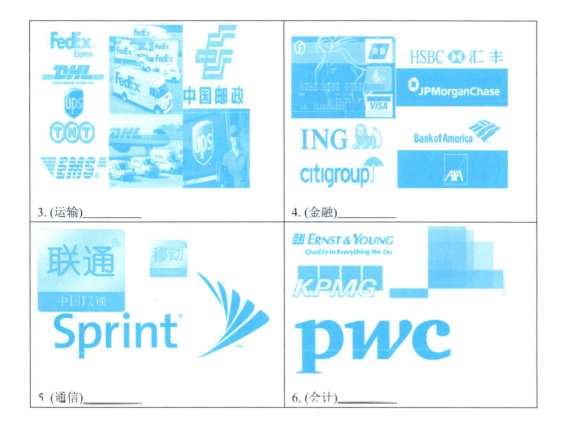

3. (运输)_____   4. (金融)_____

5. (通信)_____   6. (会计)_____

MODULE 2 手不释卷

A. Read the following information about service business and its basic accounting cycle.

1. Read the notepad (shown in Exhibit 2-1) that John put on Mary's desk and discuss with your partner about "what is a service business?"

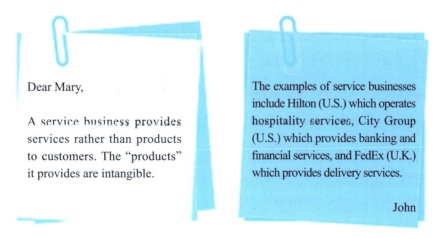

Dear Mary,

A service business provides services rather than products to customers. The "products" it provides are intangible.

The examples of service businesses include Hilton (U.S.) which operates hospitality services, City Group (U.S.) which provides banking and financial services, and FedEx (U.K.) which provides delivery services.

John

Exhibit 2-1   Service Business

UNIT 2
ACCOUNTING FOR SERVICE BUSINESS

2. Read Exhibit 2-2 and remember the "basic accounting cycle of a service business".

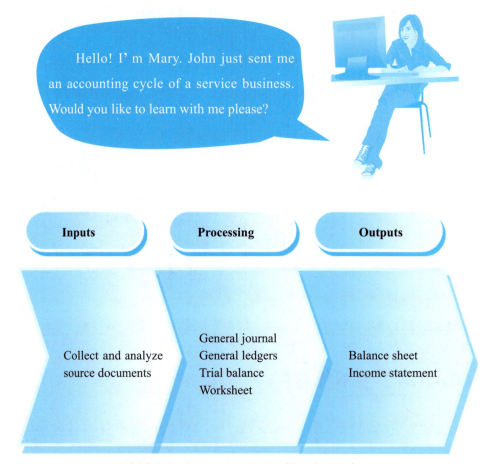

Exhibit 2-2 Accounting Cycle of Service Business

B. Learn the new words and phrases in the above passage and try to make sentences with them.

New Words

intangible	[inˈtændʒəbl]	adj. (指企业资产)无形的
hospitality	[ˌhɔspiˈtæliti]	n. (提供给客人的)食宿招待
banking	[ˈbæŋkiŋ]	n. 银行业务，银行业
financial	[faiˈnænʃl]	adj. 财政的，金融的
delivery	[diˈlivəri]	n. 递，送交

Useful Expressions and Knowledge

1. source document 原始凭证
2. general journal (GJ) 普通日记账，普通分录簿
3. general ledgers (GL) 总账
4. trial balance (TB) 试算平衡表
5. worksheet 工作表，计算表，工作底稿

worksheet在会计核算中一般翻译成工作表或计算表，在审计工作中一般翻译成工作底稿。

MODULE 3 博学多才

A. Visit the relevant website and write down some useful information you've learnt from it in English.

https://www.fortunechina.com/fortune500/c/2022-08/03/content_415683.htm

推荐理由：2022年《财富》世界500强公司简介。

_____

_____

B. Help your understanding.

服务型企业会计核算与工商企业不同

服务型企业经营形式多样，行业分布广且营业规模较小。在会计英语里，由于服务企业不同于工商企业，通常要根据企业自身的特点进行适合该企业的会计核算，不能拘泥于传统的会计核算模式。

C. 2022年世界500强前30强中的部分服务企业(见Exhibit 2-3)

排名	公司标志	中文常用名称	总部所在地	主要业务	营业收入/百万美元
11	UnitedHealth Group	联合健康集团(UnitedHealth Group)	美国	健保服务	287 597
14	BERKSHIRE HATHAWAY HomeServices	伯克希尔哈撒韦(Berkshire Hathaway)	美国	保险	276 094

Exhibit 2-3　2022年世界500强前30强中的部分服务企业

(续表)

排名	公司标志	中文常用名称	总部所在地	主要业务	营业收入/百万美元
22	ICBC 中国工商银行	中国工商银行 (Industrial & Commercial Bank of China)	中国	银行	54 003.1
24	中国建设银行 China Construction Bank	中国建设银行 (China Construction Bank)	中国	银行	46 898.9
25	中国平安 PING AN	中国平安保险 (Ping An Insurance)	中国	保险	15 753.9
28	中国农业银行 AGRICULTURAL BANK OF CHINA	中国农业银行 (Agricultural Bank of China)	中国	银行	37 390.8
30	cigna healthcare	信诺 (Cigna Healthcare)	美国	保险	5 365

Exhibit 2-3　2022年世界500强前30强中的部分服务企业(续)

RECORD TRANSACTIONS FOR SERVICE BUSINESS

GOALS 学习目标

- Journalize transactions in a two-column general journal.
- Post the transactions from the general journal to the general ledger.
- Make a trial balance statement.

MODULE 1 学以致用

Fill in the blanks with the proper Chinese expressions.

Chart of accounts (COA) is a list of all accounts used by a business. Each account in the chart is assigned a unique identifier.

Mary要为Premier广告公司进行会计记账，她向John要来了该公司的会计科目表（见Exhibit 2-4）。Mary请您帮她将Premier广告公司的英文会计科目表翻译成中文。请将会计科目的中文译文写在下面表格右边的空白栏里。

Premier Advertising Co. Chart of Accounts		
Assets		1. 例如：会计科目表
101	Cash on hand	2. _____资产_____
		3. _____
102	Cash at bank	4. _____
105	Accounts receivable	5. _____
110	Office supplies	6. _____
150	Motor vehicle	7. _____
151	Office equipment	8. _____
Liabilities		9. _____负债_____
200	Accounts payable	10. _____
Owners' Equity		11. ___所有者权益___
300	Capital	12. _____
301	Drawings	13. _____
Revenues		14. _____收入_____
400	Service revenue	15. _____
Expenses		16. _____费用_____
500	Wages expense	17. _____
501	Rent expense	18. _____

Exhibit 2-4　Chart of Accounts of Premier Advertising Co.

MODULE 2 手不释卷

A. Read the following information and learn to record transactions for service businesses.

Mary仔细阅读了Premier广告公司的会计科目表。她发现有些科目和她在中文会计里学过的工商企业会计科目不太一样。如Exhibit 2-5的电子邮件所示，John对Mary的疑惑进行了解答。

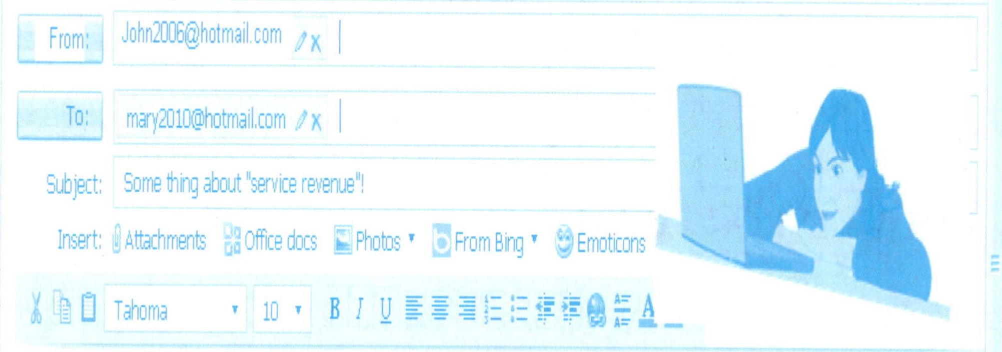
From:
John2006@hotmail.com
To:
mary2010@hotmail.com
Subject:
Some thing about "service revenue"!
Insert:
Attachments
Office docs
Photos
From Bing
Emoticons
Tahoma
10

Dear Mary,

The revenue account for the ordinary activities of a service entity is usually called service revenue (or service fee). Under the accrual basis accounting, the service revenue account reports the fees earned by a company during the time period.

The names and numbers of the accounts used in the general ledger are obtained from the chart of accounts of that particular company. Most service entities are so small that they aren't subject to strict accounting standards as those publicly listed companies are.

I hope the information above will be useful for you!

Sincerely yours,

John

Exhibit 2-5　Differences of Accounts Between Service Business and Manufacturing Business

B. Learn the new words and phrases in the above passage and try to make sentences with them.

New Words

ordinary	[ˈɔːdinəri]	adj. 普通的，平常的
account	[əˈkaunt]	n. 账，账户
obtain	[əbˈtein]	vt. 获得，得到；买到
particular	[pəˈtikjulə]	adj. 特定的，某一的
restrict	[risˈtrikt]	vt. 限制；约束

Useful Expressions and Knowledge

1. service revenue 服务收入，劳务收入
2. accrual basis accounting 权责发生制
3. be subject to 受……约束，制约
4. accounting standards 会计准则
5. publicly listed company 公开上市的公司

C. Work with your partner and learn to make journal entries.

Background: Mary is making the general journal for Premier Advertising Co. under the guidance of John. Please try to learn with Mary.

Transactions:

2022

Oct. 1   A. D. Brown invested cash of $80 000 into the advertising agency.

Oct. 2   Purchased $2 500 worth of office equipment and $500 worth of office supplies on credit.

Oct. 5   Daltrymple Icecream Company was billed $1 700 for advertising services.

Oct. 6   Paid the bill of Oct. 2 in full for the office equipment and office supplies.

Oct. 9   Purchased $16 000 worth of motor vehicle in cash.

Oct. 14   Paid staff $1 200 for work done.

Oct. 17   Received bank cheque of $1 700 from Daltrymple Icecream Company.

Oct. 21　Paid rent of $1 500 in cash for office premises.

Oct. 23　Produced advertisement for Supreme Kitchens and was paid $600 in cash.

Oct. 29　A. D. Brown withdrew $500 for personal expenses.

Directions:

(1) Work with your partner and try to understand how to record the transactions of a service business in the General Journal shown in Exhibit 2-6.

			General Journal			Page 1	
	Date		Account Name and Description	Post Ref.	Debit ($)	Credit ($)	
1	2022						1
2	Oct.	1	Cash on hand	101	80 000		2
3			Capital—A. D. Brown	300		80 000	3
4			A. D. Brown invested cash to start business				4
5		2	Office equipment	151	2 500		5
6			Office supplies	110	500		6
7			Accounts payable	200		3 000	7
8			Purchased office equipment and supplies on credit				8
9		5	Accounts receivable	105	1 700		9
10			Service revenue	400		1 700	10
11			Earned advertising service revenue				11
12		6	Accounts payable	200	3 000		12
13			Cash on hand	101		3 000	13
14			Paid bill for office equipment and supplies				14
15		9	Motor vehicle	150	16 000		15
16			Cash on hand	101		16 000	16
17			Bought motor vehicle in cash				17
18		14	Wages expense	500	1 200		18
19			Cash on hand	101		1 200	19
20			Paid staff wages				20
21		17	Cash at bank	102	1 700		21
22			Accounts receivable	105		1 700	22
23			Received a bank cheque from a customer				23

Exhibit 2-6　General Journal of Premier Advertising Co. from Oct. 1 to 17

(2) Record the remaining transactions in the following General Journal which is shown in Exhibit 2-7.

		General Journal			Page 2	
	Date	Account Name and Description	Post Ref.	Debit ($)	Credit ($)	
24	21					24
25						25
26						26
27	23					27
28						28
29						29
30	29					30
31						31
32						32
33						33
34						34

Exhibit 2-7   General Journal of Premier Advertising Co. from Oct. 21 to 29

D. Work with your partner and learn to post the transactions from the general journal to general ledgers.

Background: Mary is learning to make general ledgers on the basis of the transactions in the general journal. She has already recorded the transactions of Premier Advertising Co. from Oct. 1 to Oct. 17, 2022 (from Exhibit 2-8.1 to Exhibit 2-8.12).

Direction: Please check the general ledgers for Mary and help her record the transactions from Oct. 21 to Oct. 29, 2022.

Account Name: Cash on Hand						Account No.:101	
Date		Description	Post Ref.	Debit ($)	Credit ($)	Balance	
						Debit($)	Credit($)
2022							
Oct.	1	A. D. Brown invested cash to start business	GJ 1	80 000		80 000	
	6	Paid bill for office equipment and supplies	GJ 1		3 000	77 000	
	9	Bought motor vehicle in cash	GJ 1		16 000	61 000	
	14	Paid staff wages	GJ 1		1 200	59 800	
	21						
	23						
	29						

Exhibit 2-8.1   General Ledger of Premier Advertising Co.(1)

Account Name: Cash at Bank						Account No.:102
Date		Description	Post Ref.	Debit ($)	Credit ($)	Balance
						Debit($)	Credit($)
2022							
Oct.	17	Received a bank cheque from a customer	GJ 1	1 700		1 700	

Exhibit 2-8.2　General Ledger of Premier Advertising Co.(2)

Account Name: Accounts Receivable						Account No.:105
Date		Description	Post Ref.	Debit ($)	Credit ($)	Balance
						Debit($)	Credit($)
2022							
Oct.	5	Earned advertising service revenue	GJ 1	1 700		1 700	
	17	Received a bank cheque from a customer	GJ 1		1 700	-0-	

Exhibit 2-8.3　General Ledger of Premier Advertising Co.(3)

Account Name: Office Supplies						Account No.:110
Date		Description	Post Ref.	Debit ($)	Credit ($)	Balance
						Debit($)	Credit($)
2022							
Oct.	2	Purchased office equipment and supplies on credit	GJ 1	500		500	

Exhibit 2-8.4　General Ledger of Premier Advertising Co.(4)

Account Name: Motor Vehicle						Account No.:150
Date		Description	Post Ref.	Debit ($)	Credit ($)	Balance
						Debit($)	Credit($)
2022							
Oct.	9	Bought motor vehicle in cash	GJ 1	16 000		16 000	

Exhibit 2-8.5　General Ledger of Premier Advertising Co.(5)

Account Name: Office Equipment					Account No.:151	
Date		Description	Post Ref.	Debit ($)	Credit ($)	Balance
						Debit($)	Credit($)
2022							
Oct.	2	Purchased office equipment and supplies on credit	GJ 1	2 500		2 500	

Exhibit 2-8.6   General Ledger of Premier Advertising Co.(6)

Account Name: Accounts Payable						Account No.:200	
Date		Description	Post Ref.	Debit ($)	Credit ($)	Balance	
						Debit($)	Credit($)
2022							
Oct.	2	Purchased office equipment and supplies on credit	GJ 1		3 000		3 000
	6	Paid bill for office equipment and supplies	GJ 1	3 000			-0-

Exhibit 2-8.7   General Ledger of Premier Advertising Co.(7)

Account Name: Capital—A. D. Brown						Account No.:300	
Date		Description	Post Ref.	Debit ($)	Credit ($)	Balance	
						Debit($)	Credit($)
2022							
Oct.	1	A. D. Brown invested cash to start business	GJ 1		80 000		80 000

Exhibit 2-8.8   General Ledger of Premier Advertising Co.(8)

Account Name: Drawings—A. D. Brown						Account No.:301	
Date		Description	Post Ref.	Debit ($)	Credit ($)	Balance	
						Debit($)	Credit($)
2022							
Oct.	29						

Exhibit 2-8.9   General Ledger of Premier Advertising Co.(9)

Account Name: Service Revenue						Account No.:401	
Date		Description	Post Ref.	Debit ($)	Credit ($)	Balance	
						Debit($)	Credit($)
2022							
Oct.	5	Earned advertising service revenue	GJ 1		1 700		1 700
	23						

Exhibit 2-8.10   General Ledger of Premier Advertising Co.(10)

Account Name: Wages Expense						Account No.:500	
Date		Description	Post Ref.	Debit ($)	Credit ($)	Balance	
						Debit($)	Credit($)
2022							
Oct.	14	Paid staff wages	GJ 1	1 200		1 200	

Exhibit 2-8.11   General Ledger of Premier Advertising Co.(11)

Account Name: Rent Expense						Account No.:501	
Date		Description	Post Ref.	Debit ($)	Credit ($)	Balance	
						Debit($)	Credit($)
2022							
Oct.	21						

Exhibit 2-8.12   General Ledger of Premier Advertising Co.(12)

E. Work with your partner and try to make a trial balance statement for Premier Advertising Co.

Direction: Please try to make the trial balance statement as of Oct. 31, 2022 (shown in Exhibit 2-9) for Premier Advertising Co. on the basis of the above information.

\multicolumn{4}{c}{**Premier Advertising Co.**}

Account No.	Account Name	Debit	Credit
101			
102			
105			
110			
150			
151			
200			
300			
301			
400			
500			
501			
		82 300	82 300

Exhibit 2-9 Blank Trial Balance of Premier Advertising Co.

F. Test your understanding.

1. A trial balance might not balance because (   ).

    A. a transaction might be missed

    B. a transaction might be recorded twice

    C. a debit and credit entry might be swapped

    D. None of the above

2. On a trial balance, (   ).

    A. the total of asset accounts equals the total of liability and owners' equity accounts

    B. only the total expenses and revenues are listed

    C. the total of asset and revenue accounts equals the total of liability, expense, and equity accounts

    D. the total of asset and expense account balance equals the total of liability, revenue, and owners' equity account balance

    E. None of the above

3. Yugi enters into the following transactions in his first month of trading. What is the total entry on the debit side of the cash T account? (   )

    A. Bought $380 worth of goods in cash.   B. Paid $20 for sundry expenses.

    C. Made $1 000 in sales.   D. Received a bank loan of $5 000.

E. Paid $2 600 for fixtures and fittings.

4. Andy had accounts receivable of $4 500 at the start of 2021. On Dec. 31, 2021 he made credit sales of $45 000 and received cash of $46 500 from credit customers. What was the balance on the receivable account on Dec. 31, 2021? (　　)

   A. $6 000 Dr　　　B. $6 000 Cr　　　C. $3 000 Dr　　　D. $3 000 Cr

5. Mr. Odd had $7 800 invested in his business at the start of the year. During the course of the year he took $3 100 of cash out of the business for himself and also paid his wife, who did some secretarial work for the business, $500. The business's overall profit for the year was $8 900. Mr. Odd also paid $350 for a new personal suit using the business cheque book during the year. What is the balance on the capital account at the end of the year? (　　)

   A. $12 750　　　B. $13 250　　　C. $13 600　　　D. $13 100

MODULE 3 博学多才

A. Help your understanding.

1. 上市公司

西方国家/地区常将上市公司称为publicly listed company，或直接用PLC来表示这样的企业。企业上市一般用listing来表示(例如，listing on NYSE 指在美国纽约证券交易所上市)。如果一个公司要改制成由公众持股的公司，英语中一般用go public floating 来表示。

2. 记账要以会计科目表为指导

服务企业通常有适合各自经营特点的会计科目表(chart of accounts)，会计人员按照该企业提供的会计科目表来进行账务处理便可。以Premier广告公司为例，我们一般将办公用品(office supplies)当作当期损益计入管理费用账户，在Premier广告公司的会计科目表中将其纳入资产范畴。像机动车辆(motor vehicle)、办公设备(office equipment)这样的科目，在我国一般归入固定资产科目(fixed assets)，但Premier广告公司将这些资产科目逐一列出。

3. 记账要符合当地社会特点和习惯

由于各国/地区情况不同，有些账务的处理也体现出地区差异。以工资为例，不同国家/地区的薪酬发放方式不同：我国一般每月发一次工资，加拿大和美国的很多企业两个星期发一次工资，英国的服务企业(如酒店、餐饮企业等)一般一个星期发一次工资，澳大利亚企业一般也是一个星期发一次工资。

所以，在会计英语里，计量工资的科目有时包括工资费用 (wages expense)和应付工资 (wages payable or accrued wages)，前者属于费用 (expense)科目，后者属于流动负债(current liability)科目。

B. Sample invoice for a service business (shown in Exhibit 2-10).

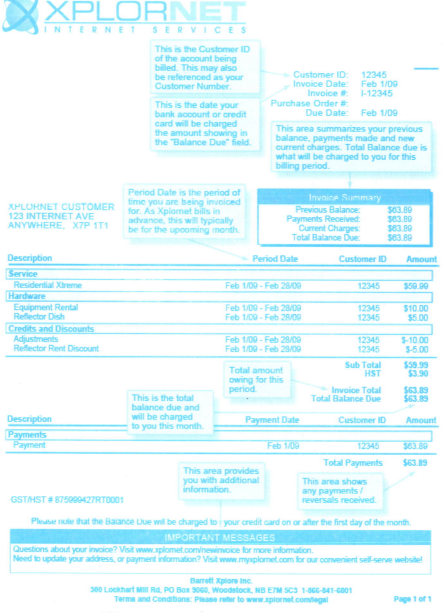

Exhibit 2-10　Sample Invoice for a Service Business

PROJECT 2

1. Background: Better Copy Service is a company providing copy service. The trial balance of this company as of May 31, 2022 and its transactions in Jun. 2022 are listed below.

Tasks:

(1) Enter the opening balance into the general ledger accounts on the basis of the trial balance as of May 31, 2022 for Better Copy Service.

(2) Record the transactions of Better Copy Service which happened in Jun. 2022 in the general journal.

(3) Post the transactions in the general journal to the general ledger.

(4) Prepare the trial balance as of Jun. 30, 2022 for Better Copy Service.

Transactions and Relevant Information:

(1) The trial balance of Better Copy Service as of May 31, 2022 was as follows (see Exhibit 2-11).

\multicolumn{4}{c}{BETTER COPY SERVICE}

Account No.	Account Name	Debit	Credit
100	Cash at bank	22 000	
105	Accounts receivable	7 000	
110	Photocopying supplies	700	
150	Equipment	15 000	
155	Motor vehicle	16 200	
200	Accounts payable		7 800
300	Capital—R. Xerox		46 950
305	Drawings—R. Xerox	250	
400	Photocopying fees		43 000
500	Supplies used	8 200	
505	Vehicle expenses	6 200	
510	Wages	18 000	
515	Office expenses	4 200	
		97 750	97 750

Exhibit 2-11 Trial Balance Statement

(2) Business transactions for the month of Jun. 2022.

2022

Jun. 5　Purchased photocopying supplies for $150 (Chq. No. 334)

Jun. 8　Cash fees for photocopying—$50 (Rec. No. 445)

Jun. 10　Receipts from debtor—$4 000 (Rec. No. 446)

Jun. 12　Billed customers for photocopying services—$8 000 (Inv. No. 1211)

Jun. 14　Cash fees for photocopying—$80 (Rec. No. 447)

　　　　Paid fortnightly accounts

　　　　• Vehicle expenses—$250 (Chq. No. 335)

　　　　• Wages—$1 000 (Chq. No. 336)

　　　　• Office expenses—$310 (Chq. No. 337)

Jun. 17　Paid $7 000 owing to the creditors (Chq. No. 338)

Jun. 20　Purchased photocopying supplies—$500 (Inv. No. 2931)

Jun. 23　Cash fees for photocopying—$110 (Rec. No. 448)

Jun. 24　Drawings by the owner

　　　　• Cash—$100 (Chq. No. 339)

　　　　• Supplies—$40 (memo 12)

Jun. 27　Billed customers for photocopying services—$7 800 (Inv. No. 1212)

Jun. 28　Paid fortnightly accounts

　　　　• Vehicle expenses—$210 (Chq. No. 340)

　　　　• Wages—$1 000 (Chq. No. 341)

　　　　• Office expenses—$290 (Chq. No. 342)

Jun. 29　Purchased photocopying supplies—$600 (Inv. No. 304)

Jun. 30　Photocopying supplies used for the month—$710 (memo 13)

Directions:

(1) Enter the opening balance from the trial balance as of May. 31, 2022 into the appropriate general ledger accounts (from Exhibit 2-12.1 to Exhibit 2-12.13).

Cash at Bank ($)　　　　　　　　　　　　　　　　　　　　　　　　　Account No.: 100

Date	Explanation	P. R.	Debit	Credit	Balance	
					Debit	Credit
2022 Jun. 1	Opening balance					

Exhibit 2-12.1　General Ledger(1)

Accounts Receivable ($)   Account No.: 105

Date	Explanation	P. R.	Debit	Credit	Balance	
					Debit	Credit
2022 Jun. 1	Opening balance					

Exhibit 2-12.2   General Ledger(2)

Photocopying Supplies ($)   Account No.: 110

Date	Explanation	P. R.	Debit	Credit	Balance	
					Debit	Credit
2022 Jun. 1	Opening balance					

Exhibit 2-12.3   General Ledger(3)

Equipment ($)   Account No.: 150

Date	Explanation	P. R.	Debit	Credit	Balance	
					Debit	Credit
2022 Jun. 1	Opening balance					

Exhibit 2-12.4   General Ledger(4)

Motor Vehicle ($)   Account No.: 155

Date	Explanation	P. R.	Debit	Credit	Balance	
					Debit	Credit
2022 Jun. 1	Opening balance					

Exhibit 2-12.5   General Ledger(5)

Accounts Payable ($)   Account No.: 200

Date	Explanation	P. R.	Debit	Credit	Balance	
					Debit	Credit
2022 Jun. 1	Opening balance					

Exhibit 2-12.6   General Ledger(6)

Capital—R. Xerox ($)   Account No.: 300

Date	Explanation	P. R.	Debit	Credit	Balance Debit	Balance Credit
2022 Jun. 1	Opening balance					

Exhibit 2-12.7   General Ledger(7)

Drawings—R. Xerox ($)   Account No.: 305

Date	Explanation	P. R.	Debit	Credit	Balance Debit	Balance Credit
2022 Jun. 1	Opening balance					

Exhibit 2-12.8   General Ledger(8)

Photocopying Fees ($)   Account No.: 400

Date	Explanation	P. R.	Debit	Credit	Balance Debit	Balance Credit
2022 Jun. 1	Opening balance					

Exhibit 2-12.9   General Ledger(9)

Supplies Used ($)   Account No.: 500

Date	Explanation	P. R.	Debit	Credit	Balance Debit	Balance Credit
2022 Jun. 1	Opening balance					

Exhibit 2-12.10   General Ledger(10)

Vehicle Expenses ($)   Account No.: 505

Date	Explanation	P. R.	Debit	Credit	Balance Debit	Balance Credit
2022 Jun. 1	Opening balance					

Exhibit 2-12.11   General Ledger(11)

Wages ($)   Account No.: 510

Date	Explanation	P. R.	Debit	Credit	Balance	
					Debit	Credit
2022 Jun. 1	Opening balance					

Exhibit 2-12.12   General Ledger(12)

Office Expenses ($)   Account No.: 515

Date	Explanation	P. R.	Debit	Credit	Balance	
					Debit	Credit
2022 Jun. 1	Opening balance					

Exhibit 2-12.13   General Ledger(13)

(2) Record the transactions of Jun. 2022 into the general journal.

BETTER COPY SERVICE
General Journal ($)   Page 21

Date		Explanation	P. R.	Debit	Credit
2022					
Jun.	5				
	8				
	10				
	12				
	14				
	17				
	20				
	23				
	24				
	27				

Exhibit 2-13   General Journal

(3) Post the transactions to the general ledger (from Exhibit 2-12.1 to Exhibit 2-12.13).

(4) Prepare the trial balance as of Jun. 30, 2022 (Exhibit 2-14).

BETTER COPY SERVICE
Trial Balance as of Jun. 30, 2022 ($)

Account No.	Account Name	Debit	Credit
100			
105			
110			
150			
155			
200			
300			
305			
400			
500			
505			
510			
515			
	Total		

Exhibit 2-14　Trial Balance

2. Background: Mr. S. Bend is running S. Bend Plumbing Co. The transactions of this company which happened in Jan. 2022 and some of the accounts are listed below.

Tasks:

(1) Prepare the general journal entries for the transactions of Jan. 2022, post the transactions to the general ledger, and prepare an unadjusted trial balance.

(2) Make the balance day adjustments, post the transactions of Jan. 2022 to the general ledger, and prepare an adjusted trial balance.

(3) Prepare a profit report for Jan. 2022 and a statement of financial position as of Jan. 31, 2022 for S. Bend Plumbing.

Transactions and Relevant Information:

◆ Assets and liabilities as of Jan. 1, 2022

Accounts payable	$150
Cash at bank	$450
Motor vehicle	$7 200
Accounts receivable	$600
Stock of materials	$500

✧ The following transactions relate to the month of Jan. 2022.

2022

Jan. 1	Paid 3 months' rent in advance—$600 (Cheque No. 6470)
	Purchased materials on credit—$600 (Inv. No. 8102)
Jan. 4	Paid $30 for petrol and oil etc. (Cheque No. 6471)
Jan. 10	Received $850 on completion of job (Rec. No. 331)
Jan. 11	Purchased $900 worth of materials in cash(Cheque No. 6472)
Jan. 16	Received $400 on account from A. Jones for job done in Dec. (Rec. No. 332)
Jan. 18	Paid $80 for petrol and oil (Cheque No. 6473)
Jan. 18	Purchased materials on credit—$700 (Inv. No. 8811)
Jan. 23	Received cash on completion of job—$500 (Rec. No. 333)
Jan. 29	Completed a major job for a builder and received $3 800 (Inv. No. 411)
Jan. 30	Cashed a cheque of $300 for personal use (Cheque No. 6474)
Jan. 31	Paid creditor $200 (Cheque No. 6475)
Jan. 31	Received $500 from P. Smith for a job—one quarter completed. The remaining three quarters will be completed in Feb.

✧ Additional Information

Jan. 31	Unused materials on hand—$450
	Wages owing—$300

Directions and Relevant Tables:

(1) Prepare the general journal (Exhibit 2-15) entries for the above transactions (ignore any balance day adjustments, and post referencing and narrations), post the transactions to the general ledger (from Exhibit 2-16.1 to Exhibit 2-16.15), and then extract an unadjusted trial balance (Exhibit 2-17).

S. BEND Plumbing
General Journal ($)

Date	Explanation	P. R.	Debit	Credit

Exhibit 2-15　General Journal

(2) Prepare the necessary general journal entries for the balance day adjustments, post the transactions to the general ledger, and extract an adjusted trial balance (Exhibit 2-18).

Cash at Bank ($)

2022						
Jan.	1	Balance				450 DR

Exhibit 2-16.1   General Ledger(1)

Accounts Receivable ($)

2022						
Jan.	1	Balance				600 DR

Exhibit 2-16.2   General Ledger(2)

Stock of Materials ($)

2022						
Jan.	1	Balance				500 DR

Exhibit 2-16.3   General Ledger(3)

Prepaid Rent ($)

Exhibit 2-16.4   General Ledger(4)

Motor Vehicle ($)

2022						
Jan.	1	Balance				7 200 DR

Exhibit 2-16.5   General Ledger(5)

Accounts Payable ($)

2022						
Jan.	1	Balance				150 CR

Exhibit 2-16.6   General Ledger(6)

Fees Received in Advance ($)

Exhibit 2-16.7　General Ledger(7)

Accrued Wages ($)

Exhibit 2-16.8　General Ledger(8)

Capital—S. Bend ($)

2022					
Jan. 1	Balance				8 600 CR

Exhibit 2-16.9　General Ledger(9)

Drawings—S. Bend ($)

Exhibit 2-16.10　General Ledger(10)

Fees Revenue ($)

Exhibit 2-16.11　General Ledger(11)

Rent ($)

Exhibit 2-16.12　General Ledger(12)

Petrol and Oil ($)

Exhibit 2-16.13　General Ledger(13)

Materials Used ($)

Exhibit 2-16.14   General Ledger(14)

Wages ($)

Exhibit 2-16.15   General Ledger(15)

S. BEND PLUMBING
Unadjusted Trial Balance as of Jan. 31, 2022 ($)

Account Name	Debit	Credit
Cash at bank		
Accounts receivable		
Stock of materials		
Prepaid rent		
Motor vehicles		
Accounts payable		
Fees received in advance		
Accrued wages		
Capital—S. Bend		
Drawings—S. Bend		
Fees revenue		
Rent		
Petrol and oil		
Materials used		
Wages		

Exhibit 2-17   Unadjusted Trial Balance

S. BEND PLUMBING
Adjusted Trial Balance as of Jan. 31, 2022 ($)

Account Name	Debit	Credit
Cash at bank		
Accounts receivable		
Stock of materials		
Prepaid rent		
Motor vehicles		
Accounts payable		
Fees received in advance		
Accrued wages		
Capital—S. Bend		
Drawings—S. Bend		
Fees revenue		
Rent		
Petrol and oil		
Materials used		
Wages		

Exhibit 2-18   Adjusted Trial Balance

(3) Prepare a profit report for the month of Jan. (see Exhibit 2-19) and a statement of financial position as of Jan. 31, 2022 (see Exhibit 2-20).

S. BEND PLUMBING STATEMENT OF FINANCIAL PERFORMANCE
FOR MONTH OF JAN. 2022 ($)

Revenue

    Fees

Less Expenses

    Rent

    Petrol and oil

    Materials used

    Wages　　　　　_____　_____

    NET PROFIT　　_____　_____

Exhibit 2-19   Statement of Financial Performance

S. BEND PLUMBING Statement of Financial Position as of Jan. 31, 2022

Current Assets		**Current Liabilities**	
Cash at bank		Accounts payable	
Accounts receivable		Fees received in advance	
Stock of materials		Accrued wages	
Prepaid rent			
Non-Current Assets		**Owners' Equity**	
Motor vehicles		Capital—S. Bend	
		Add profit	
		Less drawings	
Total assets		Total liabilities & Owners' equity	

Exhibit 2-20   Statement of Financial Position

UNIT 3

ACCOUNTING FOR MERCHANDISING BUSINESS

您好!
我是BPT贸易公司的会计Monica。欢迎您跟着我学习"商业企业的会计核算",希望我的讲解能使您有较大的收获!

Goals 学习目标

- Have general knowledge of the operating cycle of a merchandising business.
- Analyze and record purchase transactions for a merchandising business.
- Analyze and record sales transactions for a merchandising business.

Guidance 学习指导

党的二十大报告指出:"完善产权保护、市场准入、公平竞争、社会信用等市场经济基础制度,优化营商环境。"商业企业是指从事商品流通(买卖)的独立核算企业,主要包括从事粮食买卖、物资供销、对外贸易和图书发行等的企业。商业企业的商品流通环节涵盖购入、储存、销售等。其购进的商品经过整理、包装后,直接以原性能状态进行销售,因此以"库存商品"入账。

不同类型的商业企业有着各自的经营特点,对会计核算方法的要求也不同。因为商品流通企业的经济活动主要是购、销、存活动,所以这类企业的会计核算通常侧重于采购成本和销售成本的核算及商品流通费用的核算。

MERCHANDISING BUSINESS AND ITS OPERATING CYCLE

GOALS 学习目标

- Get familiar with merchandising businesses and the operating cycle of merchandising businesses.
- Have general knowledge of the distinct features of the accounting system of a merchandising business.
- Be able to name a few famous merchandising businesses and get familiar with them.

MODULE 1 学以致用

Look at the pictures and match them with the correct words in the box.

| package | storage | purchase | sale |

1. (采购)_____

2. (仓储)_____

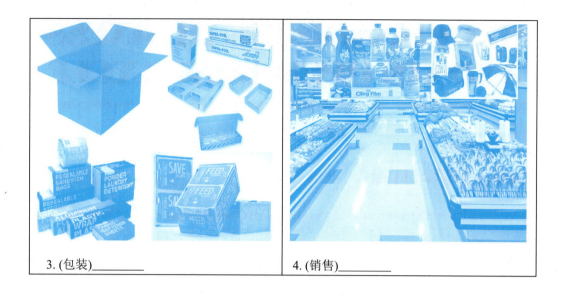

3. (包装)_____   4. (销售)_____

MODULE 2 手不释卷

A. Read the following information about merchandising business and its operating cycle.

A merchandising business is one that buys and sells goods in order to make a profit. The goods that a company buys in order to resell are known as merchandise. Before it can be sold, the merchandise must be purchased. The seller of merchandise is commonly known as the vendor and the source document for a purchase of merchandise is the purchase invoice.

1. Operating Cycle of a Merchandising Business

The major operational activities of a merchandising business are purchases and sales of merchandise.

A merchandising company begins its operation with purchases of goods from other businesses (such as manufacturers, wholesalers, distributors etc.), and earns sales revenue through sales of merchandise.

2. Typical Accounts Relevant to Merchandise Operations

◆ Merchandise inventory: the goods held for resale in the normal course of business.

◆ Sales revenue: the revenue from selling of merchandise.

◆ Cost of merchandise sold (COMS): the expense of buying and preparing merchandise inventory for resale.

B. Learn the new words and phrases in the above passage and try to make sentences with them.

New Words

merchandise	[ˈmɜːtʃəndaɪz]	n. 商品，货物；vt. 买卖，经营
purchase	[ˈpɜːtʃəs]	vt. 采购，购买
manufacture	[ˌmænjuˈfæktʃə]	vt. 制造
wholesaler	[ˈhəulseilə]	n. 批发商
distributor	[disˈtribjutə]	n. 分销商
inventory	[ˈinvəntəri]	n. 存货
prepare	[priˈpɛə]	vt. 准备

Useful Expressions and Knowledge

1. merchandise inventory 库存商品

商业企业购入的产品在包装后可直接用于销售，这样的产品在商业企业中叫库存商品 (merchandise inventory)。生产企业购入的是原材料 (raw material)，需要将其加工成可供销售的产成品 (finished products)。

2. sales revenue 销售收入

服务企业的收入 (revenue) 计入劳务收入 (service revenue) 或劳务费 (service fee) 科目；商业企业和工业企业销售产品取得的收入计入销售收入 (sales revenue) 科目。在我国，一般用"主营业务收入"科目来记账。

3. cost of merchandise sold(COMS) 商品销售成本

MODULE 3 博学多才

A. Visit the relevant website and write down some useful information you've learnt from it in English.

https://doc.mbalib.com/view/e919d4b47aeaf14075180c002664a1a3.html

推荐理由：比较全面的英文商业企业会计核算讲义。

_____

_____

B. 2022年世界500强前30强中的部分商业企业(见Exhibit 3-1)

排名	公司标志	中文常用名称	总部所在地	主要业务	营业收入/百万美元
1	Walmart	沃尔玛 (Walmart Inc.)	美国	一般商品零售	572 754
10	CVS Health	CVS Health (CVS Health)	美国	药品零售	292 111
16	McKESSON	麦克森 (McKesson)	美国	保健品批发	263 966
21	AmerisourceBergen	美源伯根 (AmerisourceBergen)	美国	药品批发	213 988.8
26	COSTCO WHOLESALE	开市客 (Costco Wholesale)	美国	仓储批发	195 929

Exhibit 3-1　2022年世界500强前30强中的部分商业企业

LESSON 2
RECORD PURCHASE TRANSACTIONS FOR MERCHANDISING BUSINESS

GOALS 学习目标

- Be able to analyze purchase transactions for a merchandising business.
- Be able to distinguish cash purchases from credit purchases.
- Be able to record purchase transactions for a merchandising business.

MODULE 1 学以致用

Fill in the blanks with the proper words and expressions given below, and change the form if necessary.

| A. return | B. amount | C. credit purchase |
| D. discount | E. purchase invoice | F. cash purchase |

1. _____(现购) requires immediate cash payment.

2. _____(赊购) allows the purchasers to make payment within a certain period of time rather than pay money at the point of purchase transaction.

3. _____(采购发票) would be payable within thirty days of receipt.

4. We usually get 3% _____(折扣) from the European exporters.

5. He owed me £1 000 but could only pay half that _____(数额).

6. When will you _____(归还) my car key?

MODULE 2 手不释卷

A. Read the following information and learn to record purchase transactions for a merchandising business.

According to the terms of payment, purchase can be divided into cash purchase and credit purchase.

1. Cash Purchase

A cash purchase requires immediate cash payment at the time of purchase. See the following sample journal entry to record a cash purchase on the basis of purchase invoice.

Dr: Merchandise inventory $ (amount on purchase invoice)
   Cr: Cash at bank (or cash on hand) $ (amount on purchase invoice)

2. Credit Purchase

A credit purchase allows the purchaser to make payment within a certain period of time in the future. This period is called the credit period. See the following sample journal entry to record a credit purchase on the basis of purchase invoice.

Dr: Merchandise inventory $ (amount on purchase invoice)
   Cr: Accounts payable $ (amount on purchase invoice)

3. Discounts

There are two types of discounts: trade discounts and early settlement discounts.

1) Trade Discounts

Trade discounts are given to increase the volume of sales being made by the supplier. By reducing the selling price, buying items in bulk then becomes more attractive. For example, if Company A buys over 1000 items, the supplier might be able to drop the price of those items by 5%.

Accounting for trade discounts: deduct the trade discount at the point of sale, record the net transaction amount, and do not record the trade discount separately.

2) Early Settlement Discounts

Early settlement discounts encourage people to pay for items sooner. If a buyer pays for the goods within a set time limit, it will receive $a\%$ discount. For example, a cash discount of 3% is offered to any customers who pay within 14 days.

Accounting for settlement discounts: for the supplier who gives its customers a discount—record as discount allowed (or as sales discount); for the buyer who receives a discount from a supplier—record as discount received (or directly deduct the amount of discount from the purchase price).

A seller may offer the buyer credit terms that include a discount for early payment. This discount is an early settlement discount as we mentioned before. It is referred to as the purchase discount to the buyer. In this book, we account this discount as the reduction of the cost of merchandise purchased.

Dr: Accounts payable—Soft Co. $ (amount on purchase invoice)

   Cr: Merchandise inventory—Sand discs $ (amount of the discount)

      Cash at bank $ (amount paid to the supplier)

4. Purchase Returns and Allowances

There are two types of return: a purchase return is return outwards, while a sales return is return inwards.

Defective or unsatisfactory merchandise returned to the seller (purchase returns) or allowances granted by the seller (purchase allowances) for the merchandise are recorded in the purchase returns and allowances account. As to the seller, it is referred to as the sales returns and allowances.

For a cash purchase, the purchase returns and allowances account is recorded as follows.

Dr: Cash at bank (or cash on hand) $ (amount of goods returned or allowance received)

   Cr: Merchandise inventory $ (amount of goods returned or allowance received)

For a credit purchase, the purchase returns and allowances account is recorded as follows.

Dr: Accounts payable $ (amount of goods returned or allowance received)

   Cr: Merchandise inventory $ (amount of goods returned or allowance received)

B. Learn the new words and phrases in the above passage and try to make sentences with them.

New Words

divide	[di'vaid]	vt. & vi. 分，划分
immediate	[i'mi:diət]	adj. 立即的，即刻的
payable	['peiəbl]	adj. 应付的
allowance	[ə'lauəns]	n. 折让，补偿
defective	[di'fektiv]	adj. 有缺陷的，残次的

Useful Expressions and Knowledge

1. according to 依照，根据……
2. on the basis of 以……为根据，在……基础上
3. purchase invoice 采购发票
4. a certain period of time 一定的时间
5. credit period 信用期

信用期是销售方允许客户赊购的账期。例如，某项交易中销售方给客户30天的信用期，指客户应在该交易的发票日期后30天内还款。

6. cost of merchandise 商品成本

cost在日常英语中有成本、费用、付出(代价)等意思。在会计英语中，cost通常翻译成"成本"，而会计中的"费用"通常用expense 来表示。

7. purchase returns and allowances 采购退回与折让
8. refer to 指(的是)，把……归类为

C. Test your understanding.

Some purchase transactions of BPT Co. which happened in Jan. 2022 are listed below. Please record these transactions into BPT's general journal on the basis of what you have learnt.

1. Cash Purchase and Credit Purchase

Transaction 1 Cash Purchase

On Jan. 6, 2022, BPT Co. purchased $80 000 worth of video discs from Brown Tech Co. ; the amount was paid immediately in cash. Please record this transaction in the general journal.

Transaction 2 Credit Purchase

On Jan. 9, 2022, BPT Co. purchased $120 000 worth of flash discs from Tomas Co. on credit. Please record this transaction in the general journal.

2. Purchase Discount

Transaction 3 Credit Purchase

On Jan. 12, 2022, BPT Co. purchased $150 000 worth of sand discs from Soft Co., with purchase term of 1/15, n/30. Please record this transaction in the general journal.

Transaction 4 Amount Paid Within the Discount Period

On Jan. 18, 2022, BPT Co. paid off the amount of $150 000 by bank cheque No.131.

Please record this transaction in the general journal.

3. Purchase Return and Allowance

Transaction 5　Purchase Return and Remittance

On Jan. 21, BPT Co. returned $2 000 worth of defective sand discs back to Soft Co. and received $2 000 of remittance from Soft Co. Please record this transaction in the general journal.

MODULE 3 博学多才

A. Help your understanding.

采购折扣

折扣(discount)包括商业折扣(trade discount)和结算折扣(settlement discount)。会计英语中所说的采购折扣(purchase discount)是指销售方为敦促顾客尽早付清货款而提供的一种价格优惠。例如，假设A公司从B公司采购30 000元的商品，对方允许的付款条件为2/10，n/30。如果A公司在10日内付款，只需要付29 400元；如果在30天内付款，则必须付全额30 000元。

采购方获得的采购折扣可用来冲减商品(或材料)的采购成本，也可先记入采购折扣或购货折扣(discount received)账户。

这一折扣对于销售方来说是销售折扣(sales discount)或现金折扣，在我国，一般将现金折扣计入财务费用(financial expense)科目。在会计英语中，有些企业将这种现金折扣看作销售收入(sales revenue)的减少，直接冲减当期的销售收入，使毛利润减少；也有企业将该种折扣看作一般费用，使净利润减少。

B. Document related to purchase return and allowance.

Look at Exhibit 3-2, which shows a sample debit/credit memo. When there is purchase return or allowance, the buyer usually sends the seller a debit memo, informing the seller of the amount the buyer proposes to decrease, and stating the reasons for the return or the request for a price reduction.

SEYMOUR INDUSTRIAL SUPPLIES INC.
1735 Higginsworth Drive
Gananoque, ON H2C 2EG

Tel. (723) 852-3879 Fax. (723) 853-6496

DEBIT/CREDIT MEMO

☐ DEBIT
☐ CREDIT

DATE	ORDER NUMBER
INVOICE	SALESPERSON
SHIPPED VIA	FOB
TERMS	

TO ______________________

WE HAVE MADE THE FOLLOWING ADJUSTMENT(S) TO YOUR ACCOUNT:

QTY.	DESCRIPTION	UNIT PRICE	AMOUNT
OTHER ADJUSTMENTS			
PLEASE DEDUCT FROM ☐ OUR (DEBIT) ☐ YOUR (CREDIT)	BALANCE DUE, THIS TOTAL AMOUNT	→	

REASON FOR DEBIT/CREDIT

MERCHANDISE RECEIVED BY:

APPROVED BY:

ORIGINAL

Exhibit 3-2 Sample Debit/Credit Memo

LESSON 3

RECORD SALES TRANSACTIONS FOR MERCHANDISING BUSINESS

GOALS 学习目标

- Be able to analyze sales transactions for a merchandising business.
- Be able to distinguish cash sales from credit sales.
- Be able to record sales transactions for a merchandising business.

MODULE 1 学以致用

Fill in the blanks with the proper words and expressions given below, and change the form if necessary.

A. accounts receivable   B. cash on delivery   C. credit period
D. sales return and allowance   E. sales invoice   F. credit memo

1. Please bring the original _____(销售发票).

2. _____(销售退回与折让) is the offsetting account to sales revenue account.

3. A credit purchase allows the purchaser to make payment within the _____(信用期).

4. In the case of credit sale, when there are sales returns and allowances, the seller normally issues a _____(信用备忘录).

5. C.O.D. is the short form of _____(货到付款) under cash sales.

6. When the customer pays the amount, _____(应收账款) is decreased and cash is increased.

MODULE 2 手不释卷

A. Read the following information and learn to record sales transactions for a merchandising business.

A merchandising company earns sales revenue through sales of merchandise. Sales can be divided into cash sales and credit sales.

1. Cash Sales

Cash sales require immediate cash payment from the purchasers. Under cash sales, cash on delivery is usually abbreviated in short form "C.O.D.". See the following sample journal entry to record cash sales on the basis of sales invoice.

Dr: Cash at bank (or cash on hand) $ (amount on sales invoice)

　　Cr: Sales revenue $ (amount on sales invoice)

2. Credit Sales

Credit sales allow the purchasers to make payment within a certain period (credit period) of time after the transactions have taken place. The purchase term is usually abbreviated in short form "$1/n$, $n/30$". See the following sample journal entry to record the credit sales on the basis of sales invoice.

Dr: Accounts receivable $ (amount on sales invoice)

　　Cr: Sales revenue $ (amount on sales invoice)

When the customer pays the amount, accounts receivable is decreased and cash is increased. The journal entry can be recorded as follows.

Dr: Cash at bank (or cash on hand) $ (amount received)

　　Cr: Accounts receivable $ (amount on sales invoice)

3. Recognize the Cost of Merchandise Sold

The cost of merchandise sold is recorded at the time when the sale happens. The journal entry is recorded as follows.

Dr: Cost of merchandise sold $ (cost of merchandise sold)

　　Cr: Merchandise inventory $ (cost of merchandise sold)

4. Sales Discount

In order to encourage the buyer to pay before the end of the credit period, the seller could offer a discount called sales discount. It is usually recorded in financial expense (or sales discount) account. The journal entry is recorded as follows.

Dr: Sales discount (or financial expense) $ (amount of discount offered)

Cash on hand (or cash at bank) $ (amount received)

Cr: Accounts receivable $ (amount on sales invoice)

5. **Sales Return and Allowance**

- Sales return is the return of the merchandise because of defects or dissatisfaction.
- Sales allowance is the reduction in the selling price of goods because of a particular problem such as breakage, quality deficiency, and incorrect quantity, etc.
- Sales return and allowance is a contra revenue account. The journal entry is recorded as follows.

   Dr: Sales return and allowance

   Cr: Cash at bank

- In the case of credit sale, when there are sales returns and allowances, the seller normally issues a credit memo to the purchaser.

B. Learn the new words and phrases in the above passage and try to make sentences with them.

New Words

abbreviate	[əˈbriːvieit]	vt.	缩略
receivable	[riˈsiːvəbl]	adj.	应收的
offer	[ˈɔfə]	vt.	提供
deficiency	[diˈfiʃnsi]	n.	缺陷，不足
incorrect	[ˌinkəˈrekt]	adj.	错误的，不正确
offset	[ˈɔːfˌset]	vt.	抵消
memo	[ˈmeməu]	n.	备忘录

Useful Expressions and Knowledge

1. cash sales 现售，现销
2. credit sales 赊销
3. in short form 缩写形式
4. take place 发生

5. sales discount 销售折扣
6. in the case of 至于……，就……来说
7. sales return and allowance 销售退回与折让
8. contra account 抵销账户，备抵账户
9. credit memo 贷项凭单，付款通知

C. Test your understanding.

Some sales transactions of BPT Co. which happened in Jan. 2022 are listed below. Please record these transactions into BPT's general journal on the basis of what you have learnt.

Transaction 1 Cash Sales

On Jan. 14, 2022, BPT Co. sold video discs to Epping College for $40 000 (C.O.D.), and the price on the sales invoice was $60 000. Please record this transaction in the general journal.

Transaction 2 Credit Sales

On Jan. 23, 2022, BPT Co. sold merchandise to Thomas Retail Co. for $90 000 (2/10, *n*/30), and the price on the sales invoice was $130 000. Please record this transaction in the general journal.

Transaction 3 Sales Discount

On Jan. 27, 2022, BPT Co. received a bank cheque from Thomas Retail Co. Please record this transaction in the general journal.

Transaction 4 Sales Return and Allowance

On Jan. 28, 2022, $500 of allowance in cash was granted to Thomas Retail Co. because of a few defective discs. Please record this transaction in the general journal.

MODULE 3 博学多才

A. Help your understanding.

现金折扣和商业折扣

现金折扣(cash discount)和商业折扣不同，商业折扣是企业根据市场供需情况或针对不同的顾客在商品标价上给予的折扣。

在我国，会计核算中确认商品销售收入的金额时，不应考虑预计可能发生的现金折扣，而应在按总价确认销售收入后直接扣除商业折扣，也就是用商业折扣直接冲减销售收入。现金折扣应在发生时计入财务费用(financial expense)，而不应冲减销售收入。

上面提到的销售折扣(sales discount)相当于我国的现金折扣，而不是商业折扣，请同学们在学习时注意。

B. Exhibit 3-3 shows a sample sales invoice for a merchandising business.

easy as
Accounting Software

TAX INVOICE

Invoice Number: 101

Date: Thursday, March 03, 2022

McMac & Sons Painters
3354 Angle Way
Heavens Helpers
Cloudville
Aberton 215874

987654321

3345 4545
mcmac@mcmacandsons.com

Business Number 123456789

To: PETER MATHEWS
55 NEW ST
KINGSVILLE

Reference: REPAINT VERANDA AND SIDING

Qty	ITEM	Unit Price	GST	Totals
15	LABOUR	35.00	3.50	577.50
1	MATERIALS	250.00	25.00	275.00

Total Excluding GST	$	775.00
Total Price Includes GST of	$	77.50
TOTAL AMOUNT PAYABLE THIS INVOICE:	**$**	**891.25**

Invoice Payable 14 Days

For and on behalf of
McMac & Sons Painters

Page 1 of 1

Exhibit 3-3 Sample Sales Invoice for Merchandising Business

PROJECT 3

1. Background: Norris has listed the transactions of her company—Norris Co. which happened in Jun. 2021.

Task: Record these transactions into the relevant ledger accounts on the basis of what you have learnt.

Transactions:

(1) Sold goods in cash for $60.

(2) Paid $400 for insurance premium by cheque.

(3) Sold goods for $250, and the customer would pay in a month.

(4) Paid $50 for petrol of the delivery van.

(5) Bought $170 worth of goods for resale on credit.

(6) Took $57 out of the business for living expenses.

(7) Bought another $40 worth of goods for resale in cash.

(8) Bought a new computer ($800) for the business.

Direction and Relevant Tables:

Complete the relevant ledger accounts (from Exhibit 3-4.1 to Exhibit 3-4.9).

Cash at Bank ($)   Account No.: 100

Date	Explanation	P. R.	Debit	Credit
2021 Jun.				

Exhibit 3-4.1　General Ledger(1)

Receivables ($)   Account No.: 110

Date	Explanation	P. R.	Debit	Credit
2021 Jun.				

Exhibit 3-4.2　General Ledger(2)

Inventory ($)   Account No.: 120

Date	Explanation	P. R.	Debit	Credit
2021 Jun.				

Exhibit 3-4.3　General Ledger(3)

Non-current Asset ($)   Account No.: 140

Date	Explanation	P. R.	Debit	Credit
2021 Jun.				

Exhibit 3-4.4   General Ledger(4)

Accounts Payable ($)   Account No.: 210

Date	Explanation	P. R.	Debit	Credit
2021 Jun.				

Exhibit 3-4.5   General Ledger(5)

Drawings ($)   Account No.: 320

Date	Explanation	P. R.	Debit	Credit
2021 Jun.				

Exhibit 3-4.6   General Ledger(6)

Sales Revenue ($)   Account No.: 400

Date	Explanation	P. R.	Debit	Credit
2021 Jun.				

Exhibit 3-4.7   General Ledger(7)

Insurance Expenses ($)   Account No.: 400

Date	Explanation	P. R.	Debit	Credit
2021 Jun.				

Exhibit 3-4.8   General Ledger(8)

Vehicle Expenses ($)   Account No.: 400

Date	Explanation	P. R.	Debit	Credit
2021 Jun.				

Exhibit 3-4.9   General Ledger(9)

2. Background: Alfie opened a new company—Alfie Trade Co. The transactions of this company which happened in Feb. 2022 are listed below.

Task: Record these transactions into the general journal on the basis of what you have learnt.

Transactions:

(1) Alfie invested $10 000 of his life savings into his business bank account.

(2) He then bought $1 000 worth of goods from Isabel (a supplier) and paid by cheque.

(3) A sale was made for $400—the customer paid by cheque.

(4) Alfie made a sale for $600 and the customer promised to pay in the future.

(5) Alfie then bought $500 worth of goods from his supplier Lam on credit.

(6) Alfie paid a telephone bill of $150 by cheque.

(7) The credit customer paid the balance on her account.

(8) Alfie paid Lam $340.

(9) Bank interest of $30 was received.

(10) A cash customer returned $20 worth of goods to Alfie for a refund.

(11) Alfie sent $100 worth of goods back to Lam.

Direction and Relevant Table:

Record the above transactions in the general journal (See Exhibit 3-5).

Alfie Trade Co. General Journal ($)				Page 1
Date	Explanation	P. R.	Debit	Credit
1				
2				
3				
4				
5				
6				
7				
8				
9				
10				
11				

Exhibit 3-5　General Journal

3. Background: Tech Trading Co. is a company specializing in retailing tech products. The transactions of this company which happened in Mar. 2022 are listed below.

Task: Record these transactions into the general journal on the basis of what you have learnt.

Transactions:

(1) On Mar. 2, 2022, Tech Trading Co. purchased $10 000 worth of video discs from Tomas Co.; the amount was paid immediately in cash.

(2) On Mar. 3, 2022, Tech Trading Co. purchased $120 000 worth of car GPS facilities from Tomas Co. on credit, with purchase term of 2/10, *n*/30.

(3) On Mar. 9, 2022, Tech Trading Co. purchased $15 000 worth of sand discs from Soft Co., with purchase term of 1/15, *n*/30.

(4) On Mar.10, Tech Trading Co. returned $2 000 worth of merchandise back to Soft Co.

(5) Tech Trading Co. paid off all debts to Tomas Co. by cheque on Mar. 15, 2022.

(6) On Mar.17, Tech Trading Co. paid off all debts to Soft Co. by bank cheque.

(7) On Mar.18, Tech Trading Co. sold $4 000 worth of video discs to EDI College (2/15, *n*/30), and the price on the sales invoice was $6 000.

(8) On Mar. 24, EDI College made a payment by bank cheque. Record the effect of the transaction in the general journal.

(9) On Mar. 29, an allowance of $120 was granted to EDI College because of a few defective discs. Tech Trading Co. sent a bank cheque to EDI College.

Direction and Relevant Table:

Record the above transactions in the general journal (see Exhibit 3-6).

Tech Trade Co. General Journal ($)				Page 1
Date	Explanation	P. R.	Debit	Credit

Exhibit 3-6　General Journal

4. Background: The transactions of Matthew Trade Co., Ltd. which happened in Jan. 2022 are listed below.

Tasks:

(1) Prepare the trial balance statement as of Jan. 31 on the basis of the transactions listed below.

(2) Prepare the income statement as of Jan. 31 for Matthew Trade Co., Ltd.

Transactions:

(1) On Jan. 1, Matthew invested $10 000 as capital by cheque.

(2) On Jan. 2, Matthew bought $4 000 worth of supplies and paid by cheque.

(3) On Jan. 4, Matthew bought a delivery van and paid $2 000 by cheque.

(4) On Jan. 10, Matthew bought $1 000 worth of cargo on credit.

(5) On Jan. 14, Matthew sold goods for $1 500 and received a cheque of that amount.

(6) On Jan. 18, Matthew sold all his remaining goods for $5 000 on credit.

(7) On Jan. 21, Matthew paid $800 to his supplier by cheque.

(8) On Jan. 23, Matthew paid rent of $200 by cheque.

(9) On Jan. 26, Matthew drew $100 for living expenses from the business bank account.

Directions and Relevant Tables:

(1) Prepare the trial balance statement (see Exhibit 3-7).

Matthew Trade Co., Ltd.
Trial Balance as of Jan. 31 2022($)

Account Name	Debit	Credit
Cash at bank		
Accounts receivable		
Inventory		
Non-current assets		
Accounts payable		
Capital		
Drawings		
Sales revenue		
Rent expense		

Exhibit 3-7　Trial Balance Statement

(2) Prepare the income statement (see Exhibit 3-8).

Matthew Trade Co., Ltd.
Income Statement as of Jan. 31, 2022($)

Sales revenue	
Opening inventory	
Add: Purchases	
Less: Closing inventory	
Gross profit	
Less: Rent expense	
NET PROFIT	

Exhibit 3-8   Income Statement

UNIT 4

ACCOUNTING FOR MANUFACTURING BUSINESS

您好!
　　我是S.T. Electronic公司财务部的负责人Jessica，我司是典型的生产企业。在这段时间，您将重点学习"工业企业的会计核算"。我特地请经验丰富的Tony来指导您。如有任何问题，您可以请教他。

Goals 学习目标

- Get familiar with the operating cycle of a manufacturing business and the distinct features of its accounting procedure.
- Analyze and prepare a proper statement of the "cost of goods manufactured".
- Analyze and record typical transactions under various circumstances for a manufacturing business.

Guidance 学习指导

　　党的二十大报告强调："坚持把发展经济的着力点放在实体经济上，推进新型工业化，加快建设制造强国、质量强国、航天强国、交通强国、网络强国、数字中国。"工业企业的生产经营活动由供应过程、生产过程、销售过程组成。在供应过程，企业用货币资金购进原材料等生产对象；在生产过程，企业通过对材料进行生产和加工制造出产品，并通过对生产费用进行归集和分配计算出生产成本；在销售过程，企业通过销售产品获得销售收入。

　　成本计算是工业企业会计核算中很重要的一项任务，主要包括对供应过程中的材料采购成本、生产过程中的生产成本和销售过程中的销售成本的计算。这对工业企业正确计算财务成果有很重要的意义。

MANUFACTURING BUSINESS AND ITS OPERATING CYCLE

GOALS 学习目标

- Get familiar with manufacturing businesses and the operating cycle of manufacturing businesses.
- Have general knowledge of the distinct features of the accounting system of a manufacturing business.
- Be able to name a few famous manufacturing businesses and get familiar with them.

MODULE 1 学以致用

Look at the pictures and fill in the blanks with correct English words.

1. 供应过程 _____

2. 生产过程 _____

3. 销售过程

MODULE 2 手不释卷

A. Read the following information about manufacturing business and its operating cycle.

1. Operating Cycle of a Manufacturing Business

The major operational activities of a manufacturing business are purchase, manufacturing, and sale of products. Examples of manufacturing businesses include China National Petroleum which produces refined oil, General Motors which produces automobiles, Nike which produces athletic shoes, Coca-cola which produces beverages, and Sony which produces stereos, televisions, and radios, etc. Most of the accounting procedures discussed in previous lessons apply equally to manufacturing businesses.

Exhibit 4-1 shows the operating cycle of a printing factory, which is a typical manufacturing business. It shows that a manufacturing business converts materials into finished products through the use of machinery and labor, and earns sales revenue by selling products manufactured.

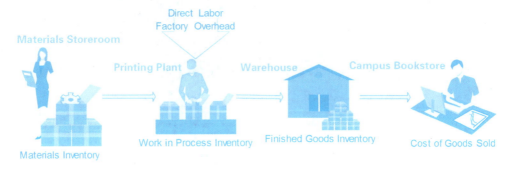

Exhibit 4-1　Sample Operating Cycle of Manufacturing Business

2. Inventory of Merchandising Business and Manufacturing Business

The merchandise held by a merchandising business is recorded as current asset called merchandise inventory. Merchandise inventory sold becomes cost of merchandise sold.

In contrast to a merchandising company, a manufacturing company has three types of inventory: materials inventory, work-in-process inventory, and finished goods inventory. The costs of work-in-process inventory include the direct materials, direct labor, and factory overhead.

The calculations of the cost of merchandise sold for a merchandising business and the cost of goods sold for a manufacturing business are respectively showed in Exhibit 4-2 and Exhibit 4-3.

Cost of Merchandise Sold	
Beginning inventory of merchandise	X
+ Purchase of merchandise	X
= Cost of merchandise available for sale	XX
− Ending inventory of merchandise	(X)
− Cost of merchandise sold	XX

Exhibit 4-2 Calculation of the Cost of Merchandise Sold

Cost of Goods Sold	
Beginning inventory of finished goods	X
+ Cost of finished goods manufactured	X
= Cost of goods available for sale	XX
− Ending inventory of finished goods	(X)
= Cost of goods sold	XX

Exhibit 4-3 Calculation of the Cost of Goods Sold

3. Three Common Inventory Cost Flow Assumptions

- ◆ First-in, first-out (FIFO) method: assumes that the first items placed in inventory warehouse are the first sold.
- ◆ Last-in, first-out (LIFO) method: assumes that the last items placed in inventory warehouse are the first sold. Look at Exhibit 4-4, which shows the difference between LIFO and FIFO.
- ◆ Average cost method: assumes that the cost of inventory is based on the average cost of the goods available for sale during the period.

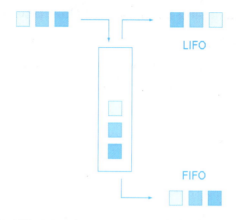

Exhibit 4-4　Flow of Items for LIFO and FIFO

B. Learn the new words and phrases in the above passage and try to make sentences with them.

New Words

previous	[ˈpriːviəs]	adj. 先前的，以前
apply	[əˈplai]	vt. 应用，使用
through	[θruː]	prep. 凭借，用
process	[ˈprəuses]	vt. 加工，处理
respectively	[risˈpektivli]	adv. 分别地

Useful Expressions and Knowledge

1. in contrast to 相比之下
2. materials inventory 材料存货
3. work-in-process inventory 在产品存货
4. finished goods inventory 产成品存货
5. direct materials 直接材料
6. direct labor 直接人工
7. factory overhead 制造费用
8. beginning inventory 期初余额
9. ending inventory 期末余额
10. first-in, first-out (FIFO) method 先进先出法

先进先出法是假定先购入的存货先领用或发出的存货计价法。

11. last-in, first-out (LIFO) method 后进先出法

后进先出法是假定后购入的存货先领用或发出的存货计价法。我国新的会计法取消了LIFO的使用。但在西方国家/地区，有大量企业选择使用LIFO，如美国的Daimler Chrysler(克莱斯勒)汽车公司、美国日用品连锁零售商KMART(卡马特)公司等。

12. average cost method 加权平均法

加权平均法是指企业以库存材料的全部数量为权数，计算存货的加权平均单位成本，以此作为发出材料存货的计价标准的一种方法。

C. Test your understanding.

1. Try to figure out different kinds of inventory with specific examples for Hershey Co.

_____

_____

2. Fill in the blanks with the proper words and expressions given below, and change the form if necessary.

A. materials inventory	B. work-in-process inventory	C. materials
D. machineries	E. finished goods inventory	F. cost of goods sold
G. current asset	H. direct labor cost	I. factory overhead
J. direct materials cost	K. cost of goods manufactured	

(1) A manufacturing business converts_____(材料) into finished products through the use of_____(机器) and labor.

(2) _____(直接材料成本) is the cost of raw materials used in manufacturing a product.

(3) _____(产成品存货) consists of the costs for fully completed products. When the finished goods are sold, the costs are transferred to the_____(销售成本).

(4) _____(在产品存货) consists of the costs for partially completed products. The costs of it include the direct materials, direct labor, and_____(制造费用).

(5) _____(直接人工成本) consists of the wages of factory workers directly involved with making a product.

(6) Inventory is reported in the balance sheet as a _____(流动资产).

MODULE 3 博学多才

A. Visit the relevant websites and write down some useful information you've learnt from it in English.

1. https://doc.mbalib.com/view/e29f89688eba007ab5142ce8be93fd99.html

   推荐理由：专业的网站，全面的工业企业会计核算英文资料。

2. https://www.docin.com/p-145064483.html

   推荐理由：较全面的工业企业会计核算中文资料。

B. Help your understanding.

后进先出法(LIFO)的缺点

Exhibit 4-5以简单易懂的方式显示了LIFO的运作方式。LIFO按照后入库的存货先发出的原则计算发出存货和期末存货的成本。其结果是，"存货"项目的金额反映的是最初取得存货的成本，因此会远离存货的最近成本，最终背离存货的实际成本，尤其是在持续通货膨胀的情况下，"后进先出法"计算的存货项目的金额不能准确地反映期末存货的实际价值。

Exhibit 4-5　Picture of LIFO

C. 2022年世界500强前20强中的部分生产企业(见Exhibit 4-6)

排名	公司标志	中文常用名称	总部所在地	主要业务	营业收入/百万美元
4		中国石油天然气 (China National Petroleum)	中国	炼油	411 692.9
5		中国石油化工 (Sinopec)	中国	炼油	401 313.5
6		沙特阿美 (Saudi Aramco)	沙特阿拉伯	炼油	400 399.1
7		苹果公司 (Apple)	美国	电子产品	365 817
8		大众公司 (Volkswagen)	德国	汽车	295 819.8
12		埃克森美孚 (Exxon Mobil)	美国	炼油	285 640
13		丰田汽车 (Toyota Motor)	日本	汽车	279 337.7
15		壳牌公司 (Shell)	英国	炼油	272 657

Exhibit 4-6　2022年世界500强前20强中的部分生产企业

LESSON 2
ANALYZE THE "COST OF GOODS MANUFACTURED"

GOALS 学习目标

- Be able to analyze the "cost of goods manufactured".
- Be able to prepare a proper statement of the "cost of goods manufactured".

MODULE 1 学以致用

Fill in the blanks with the proper words and expressions given below, and change the form if necessary.

A. indirect labor   B. insurance   C. depreciation
D. indirect materials   E. period expenses

1. _____(期间费用) are those which occur during a period of time and cannot be easily associated with products or the production process.

2. _____(间接人工) are workers (such as accountants, supervisors, security guards) who do not directly produce goods or provide service, but make their production possible or more efficient.

3. _____(间接材料) are those consumables (such as disposable tools, protective devices) not used as raw materials. Instead, they make the production possible, more efficient, or safer.

4. _____(保险) is a form of risk management primarily used to hedge against the risk of a contingent, uncertain loss.

5. _____(折旧费) is an expense recorded to allocate a tangible asset's cost over its useful life.

MODULE 2 手不释卷

A. Read the following information and learn to analyze the "cost of goods manufactured".

1. Costs Incurred During the Manufacturing Process

The costs of work-in-process inventory include the direct materials, direct labor, and factory overhead. Examples of factory overhead include indirect materials (i.e. containers) cost, indirect labor cost (i.e. supervisory salaries, maintenance workers' salaries), machine depreciation and maintenance, factory supplies and factory insurances, etc. The cost of goods manufactured is transferred to the finished goods inventory account and is used in calculating cost of goods sold.

During the process of manufacturing, a company also incurs period expenses not related to manufacturing functions, such as those related to finance, selling, and general administrative functions.

There are three period expenses: general administrative expense, financial expense, and sales expense. Examples of period expenses include rent, interest, taxes, and sales salaries, etc.

2. Flow of Costs Through Manufacturing Company (Shown in Exhibit 4-7)

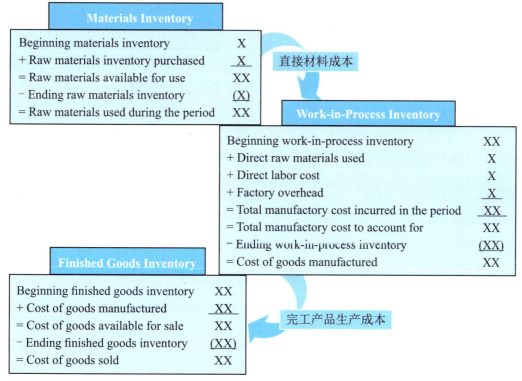

Exhibit 4-7 Flow of Costs Through Manufacturing Company

3. Schedule of Cost of Goods Manufactured

The schedule of cost of goods manufactured, which is shown in Exhibit 4-8, is used to calculate the cost of producing products.

Hedice Automobile, Inc. Cost of Goods Manufactured Schedule as of Dec. 31, 2022($)		
Direct materials used		
Beginning raw materials inventory	6 200	
Add: Cost of raw materials purchased	<u>49 400</u>	
Total raw materials available	55 600	
Less: Ending raw materials inventory	(5 800)	
Total raw materials used		49 800
Direct labor		125 600
Manufacturing overhead		
Indirect materials	4 100	
Indirect labor	43 700	
Depreciation—factory building	9 500	
Depreciation—factory equipment	5 400	
Insurance—factory	12 000	
Property taxes—factory	4 500	
Total manufacturing overhead		<u>79 200</u>
Total manufacturing costs		254 600
Add: Beginning work-in-process inventory		10 200
		264 800
Less: Ending work-in-process inventory		(9 800)
Cost of goods manufactured		255 000

Exhibit 4-8 Schedule of Cost of Goods Manufactured

B. Learn the new words and phrases in the above passage and try to make sentences with them.

New Words

adjust	[ə'dʒʌst]	vt. 调整
indirect	[ˌindi'rekt]	adj. 间接的
depreciation	[diˌpriːʃi'eiʃn]	n. (资产等)折旧
maintenance	['meintinəns]	n. 保养，维修
utility	[juː'tiliti]	n. 公共服务，如水、电等
supervisory	[ˌsjuːpə'vaizəri]	adj. 管理的，监督的
supply	[sə'plai]	n. 供给物，供应品，日用品

Useful Expressions and Knowledge

1. schedule of cost of goods manufactured 生产成本明细表
2. period expenses 期间费用
3. indirect materials cost 间接材料成本
4. indirect labor cost 间接人工成本
5. supervisory salaries 车间管理人员工资
6. factory supplies 车间日用品
7. factory insurances 工厂保险费

C. Test your understanding.

Background: Tony has provided you with the accounting data of S.T. Electronic Co. of Nov. 2022 (from Exhibit 4-9 to Exhibit 4-13). Please prepare the schedule of cost of goods manufactured of Nov. 2022 for S.T. Electronic Co.

来自Tony的提醒：并不是所有的数据都对生产成本的汇总计算有用，请注意分辨干扰信息。

Information：

Work-in-Process Inventory	Nov. 1, 2022($)	Nov. 30, 2022($)
Product 79#	12 000	4 500
Product 45#	1 000	1 500
Total	13 000	6 000

Exhibit 4-9　Work-in-Process Inventory

Materials Inventory	Material A ($)	Material B ($)	Total amount ($)
Raw materials inventory Nov. 1	9 700	19 800	29 500
Raw materials purchased	80 000	60 000	140 000
Raw materials used Product 79#	25 000	55 000	80 000
Product 45#	45 000	10 000	55 000
Total raw materials used	70 000	65 000	135 000
Raw materials inventory Nov. 30	19 700	14 800	34 500

Exhibit 4-10   Materials Inventory

Wages	Wage rate ($)	Employee No.	Total amount ($)
1. Labor for Product 79#	2 000	20	40 000
Labor for Product 45#	2 500	10	25 000
2. Production supervisory	4 000	1	4 000
3. Machinery maintenance	3 000	1	3 000
Total		32	72 000

Exhibit 4-11   Wages

Other Factory Expenses	Amount ($)
Materials	3 000
Utilities	3 000
Insurances	1 000
Supplies	1 800
Total	8 800

Exhibit 4-12   Other Factory Expenses

Depreciation Expenses	Amount ($)
Factory	2 000
Factory equipment and vehicles	1 000
General administrative facilities	1 800
Other vehicles (not in factory)	5 800
Total	10 600

Exhibit 4-13   Depreciation Expenses

Direction: Prepare a cost of goods manufactured schedule for S.T. Electronic Co. as of Nov. 30, 2022.

MODULE 3 博学多才

A. Visit the relevant website and write down some useful information you've learnt from it in English.

https://www.docin.com/p-19255055.html

推荐理由：比较直观的生产成本明细表(cost of goods manufactured schedule)的PPT演示，能帮助您理解本课的部分知识。

_____
_____

B. Help your understanding.

期间费用 (period expenses)

工业企业在生产经营过程中，除了会发生构成产品生产成本的费用外，因管理和保证生产的需要，还会产生各种不能直接归属于某个特定产品成本的期间费用(period expenses)，如营业费用(sales expense)、管理费用(general administrative expense)和财务费用(financial expense)。

LESSON 3

RECORD TRANSACTIONS FOR MANUFACTURING BUSINESS

GOALS 学习目标

- Be able to analyze various transactions for a manufacturing business.
- Be able to record typical transactions under various circumstances for a manufacturing business.

MODULE 1 学以致用

Fill in the blanks with the proper words and expressions given below, and change the form if necessary.

| deliver | destination | determine | depend |
| previous | ownership | transportation | freight |

1. He got round the _____(运输) by renting a car.
2. The author mentioned it in the _____(过去的) paragraph.
3. The house is under new _____(所有权).
4. Whether the game will be played _____(取决于) on the weather.
5. He has not _____(决定) what he will study.
6. We eventually arrived at our _____(目的地).
7. We _____(运送) the goods to the warehouse by truck.
8. The telegram was _____(投递) early this morning.

MODULE 2 手不释卷

A. Read the following information and learn to record transactions for a manufacturing business.

The major operational activities of a manufacturing business are purchase, manufacturing, and sale of products. Most of the accounting procedures discussed in the previous lessons apply equally to manufacturing businesses.

1. Transportation Costs

Does the buyer or seller pay transportation costs? It depends on when the ownership (or title) of the goods passes from the seller to the buyer. The transfer of ownership also determines whether the buyer or seller must pay other costs, such as the cost of insurance.

- ◇ FOB shipping point: the ownership of the goods passes to the buyer when the seller delivers the goods to the transportation company or freight carrier. Under this term, The buyer pays the transportation costs to the final destination.

- ◇ FOB destination: the ownership of the goods passes to the buyer when the buyer receives the goods. Under this term, the seller delivers the goods and pays the transportation costs to the buyer's final destination. Exhibit 4-14 shows the difference between FOB shipping point and FOB destination.

Exhibit 4-14   Difference Between FOB Shipping Point and FOB Destination

2. Sales Tax

Most countries charge tax on sales of goods. The liability for the sales tax is incurred when the sales is made. At regular intervals, the seller pays the amount of the sales tax collected to the tax bureau. The formula to calculate the sales tax is:

$$\text{Sales tax} = \text{Amount of sales} \times \text{Sales tax rate}$$

3. Transactions Related to Purchase

- Under cash purchase, the company should record the transaction as follows.

  Dr: Raw materials $XX

  　　Cr: Cash on hand (or cash at bank) $XX

- Under credit purchase, the company should record the transaction as follows.

  Dr: Raw materials $XX

  　　Cr: Accounts payable $XX

4. Transactions Related to Productions

The most typical transactions related to the production process include use of materials, recognizing (or paying) employees' wages, and computing the manufactory cost of finished goods completed during the period, etc. These transactions could be recorded as follows.

- Use of Materials

  Dr: Cost of goods manufactured $XXX

  　　Factory overhead $XX

  　　Cr: Raw materials $XXX

- Recognizing (or Paying) Employees' Wages

  Dr: Cost of goods manufactured $XXX

  　　Factory overhead $XX

  　　Cr: Wages payable (or cash at bank) $XXX

- Allocation of Depreciation Expenses

  Dr: General & administrative expenses $XX

  　　Factory overhead $XX

  　　Cr: Accumulated depreciation $XXX

- Allocation and Post of Factory Overhead

  Dr: Cost of goods manufactured—Product A $XX

  　　　　　　　　　　　　　—Product B $XX

  　　Cr: Factory overhead $XX

- Determining Cost of Finished Goods Completed During the Period

  Dr: Finished goods inventory $XXX

  　　Cr: Cost of goods manufactured $XX

5. Transactions Related to Sales

- Under cash sales, the company should record the transaction as follows.

    Dr: Cash on hand (or cash at bank) $XX

      Cr: Sales revenue $XX

    Dr: Cost of goods sold $XX

      Cr: Finished goods inventory $XX

- Under credit sales, the company should record the transaction as follows.

    Dr: Accounts receivable $XX

      Cr: Sales revenue $XX

    Dr: Cost of goods sold $XX

      Cr: Finished goods inventory $XX

B. Learn the new words and phrases in the above passage and try to make sentences with them.

New Words

transportation	[ˌtrænspɔːˈteiʃn]	n. 运送，运输
ownership	[ˈəunəʃip]	n. 物主的身份；所有(权)
title	[ˈtaitl]	n. 权益，权利
shipping	[ˈʃipiŋ]	n. (货物的)运输，运送
destination	[ˌdestiˈneiʃn]	n. 目的地，终点
charge	[tʃɑːdʒ]	vt. 收费，要价
interval	[ˈintəvəl]	n. 间隔时间
formula	[ˈfɔːmjulə]	n. 公式，方程式
administrative	[ədˈministrətiv]	adj. 管理的

Useful Expressions and Knowledge

1. general & administrative expenses 管理费用
2. depend on 依靠，随……而定
3. freight carrier 货物运输工具(如火车车厢、集装箱等)
4. sales tax 消费税

C. Test your understanding.

Some transactions of S.T. Electronic Co. which happened in Nov. 2022 are listed below. Please try to record these transactions into the general journal on the basis of what you have learnt.

Transaction 1

On Nov. 4, 2022, S.T. Electronic Co. bought material A from Jack&Sons Co., and the price on the invoice was $80 000, 1/10, n/30, FOB shipping point. The transportation cost of $800 was prepaid by Jack&Sons Co. Please record this transaction in the general journal.

Transaction 2

On Nov. 5, 2022, S.T. Electronic Co. bought raw material B from Potty Co. for $60 000, and the invoice was paid by bank cheque. Please record this transaction in the general journal.

Transaction 3

On Nov. 10, 2022, S.T. Electronic Co. sent a bank cheque to Jack&Sons Co. to pay off the invoice.

Transaction 4

Use the following information (from Exhibit 4-15 to Exhibit 4-17), and record the transactions in the general journal.

Materials Inventory	Material A ($)	Material B ($)	Total Amount ($)
Raw materials purchased	80 000	60 000	140 000
Raw materials used Product 79#	25 000	55 000	80 000
Product 45#	45 000	10 000	55 000

Exhibit 4-15   Materials Inventory

Wages	Wage Rate ($)	Employee No.	Total Amount ($)
1. Labor for Product 79#	2 000	20	40 000
Labor for Product 45#	2 500	10	25 000
2. Production supervisory	4 000	1	4 000
3. Machinery maintenance	3 000	1	3 000
Total		32	72 000

Exhibit 4-16   Wages

Work-in-Process Inventory	Nov. 1, 2022 ($)	Nov. 30, 2022 ($)
Product 79#	12 000	4 500
Product 45#	1 000	1 500
Total	13 000	6 000

Exhibit 4-17   Work-in-Process Inventory

Other related information:

Factory overhead not related to materials usage and employees' wages was $11 800. S.T. Electronic Co. equally (1:1) allocated the factory overhead between Product 79# and Product 45#.

Transaction 5

On Nov. 26 , 2022, S.T. Electronic Co. sold $120 000 of Product 79# and $90 000 of Product 45# to K-Mall. The amounts on the sales invoice are Product 79# $150 000 and Product 45# $125 000. K-Mall paid off the invoice by bank cheque (ignore tax). Please record this transaction in the general journal.

MODULE 3 博学多才

Help your understanding.

1. 消费税 (sales tax)

在会计英语中，sales tax相当于我国的消费税。对于sales tax，我们不能直接根据字面意思将其翻译成"销售税"或像有些翻译软件那样将它翻译为"营业税"。sales tax是对烟、酒、化妆品、汽车等少数应税消费品征收的税金。美国向生产和批发汽油、酒等商品的企业征收的货物税(excise taxes)，以及澳大利亚和加拿大等国征收的商品和服务税(goods and services tax, GST)，都属于消费税的税种。不同的消费品适用不同的税率或税额。

2. 不同企业费用的登记

对于生产、经营过程中产生的各种费用，英语国家/地区大中型企业的记账方式与我国的相似，许多小企业采用"产生什么费用，登记什么费用"的方式来入账。这和大中型企业的记账方式有所不同。

例如，某公司支付本月的厂房租金：在我国会计记账中，一般借记"制造费用"，贷记"银行存款"；在会计英语中，小企业一般直接借记rent expense(租金费用)，贷记cash at bank(银行存款)。

又如，每月的工厂机器设备等的折旧费：在我国会计记账中，一般借记"制造费用"，贷记"累计折旧"；在会计英语中，小企业一般直接借记depreciation expense(折旧费用)，贷记accumulated depreciation(累计折旧)。

PROJECT 4

Background: Handy Electronic Co. is a company specializing in developing and manufacturing tech products. The transactions of this company which happened in Jan. 2022 are listed below.

Task: Try to record these transactions into the general journal on the basis of what you have learnt.

Transactions:

1. On Jan. 9, 2022, Handy Electronic Co. purchased raw material A from Tomas Co. for production of Delta. The price on the purchase invoice was $20 000. It allowed 2% discount if the payment was made before Jan. 29, 2022, under FOB shipment. Transportation cost of $500 was prepaid by Tomas Co.

2. On Jan. 14, $400 worth of defective merchandise was returned to Tomas Co.

3. On Jan. 25, 2022, Handy Electronic Co. purchased $10 000 worth of material B from Tony Tech Co. for production of Delta; the amount was paid immediately by bank cheque.

4. On Jan. 18, Handy Electronic Co. sent a bank cheque to Tomas Co.and paid off the outstanding balance.

5. In Jan. 2022, factory of Handy Electronic Co. used $8 000 worth of raw material A and $6 000 worth of raw material B to produce 100 units of Delta. All products were completed in the month. 3 factory workers (Mike, Anna, and John) were involved in the production and incurred labor cost of $1 000, $1 100, and $900. Factory overhead cost allocated on these 100 units of Delta was $1 200 in total. Check the statement of cost of goods manufactured in Exhibit 4-18.

6. On Jan. 1, 2022, Handy Electronic Co. had 40 units of Delta in its warehouse. The cost was $190 per unit. Total sales of Delta for the month was 120 units and $400 per unit, and the company received a bank cheque of $48 000 (ignore taxes).

Handy Electronic Co. Statement of Cost of Goods Manufactured as of Jan. 31, 2022 ($)		
Beginning work-in-process inventory		3 000
Add: Direct raw materials used		
Beginning inventory	11 000	
+ Purchase of direct raw materials	29 808	
– Purchase return	(400)	
– Purchase discount	(392)	
Raw materials available for use	40 016	
Ending inventory	(26 016)	
Direct raw materials used		14 000
Direct labor		3 000
Factory overhead:		
Indirect raw materials	200	
Indirect labor	50	
Utilities	220	
Repair and maintenance	50	
Rent on plant facilities	100	
Factory supplies used	50	
Administrative salaries	300	
Insurance	30	
Depreciation on machinery and equipment	200	
Total factory overhead		1 200
Total manufactory cost incurred in the month		18 200
Total manufactory cost to account for		21 200
Less: Ending work-in-process inventory		(3 000)
Cost of goods manufactured		18 200

Exhibit 4-18   Statement of Cost of Goods Manufactured

Direction and Relevant Table: Record the transactions in the general journal (Exhibit 4-19).

Handy Electronic Co.				
General Journal				Page 1
Date	Explanation	P. R.	Debit	Credit

Exhibit 4-19   General Journal

UNIT 5

FINANCIAL STATEMENTS

您好!
　　我是史密斯会计公司的会计Susan，我正在教我的新同事Andy如何编制期末财务报表。
　　同学们，和Andy一起学习"财务报表的编制"吧!

Goals 学习目标

- Have general ideas of the financial report.
- Understand the typical format and draft a simple balance sheet.
- Understand the typical format and draft a simple income statement.
- Understand the typical format of a cash flow statement.

Guidance 学习指导

　　党的二十大报告指出："深化金融体制改革，建设现代中央银行制度，加强和完善现代金融监管，强化金融稳定保障体系，依法将各类金融活动全部纳入监管，守住不发生系统性风险底线。"企业要维持良好的财务状况，离不开国家的金融稳定保障体系，也离不开正确编制的财务会计报告。财务会计报告是指企业对外提供的反映企业某一特定日期财务状况和某一会计期间经营成果、现金流量的文件。完整的财务会计报告体系包括财务报表、财务报表附注、财务情况说明书。其中，财务报表包括基本报表和附表。基本财务报表至少应包括资产负债表、利润表、现金流量表、所有者权益(股东权益)变动表。

AN OVERVIEW OF FINANCIAL STATEMENTS

GOALS 学习目标

- Have general ideas of the financial statements.
- Get familiar with the contents and users of financial statements.

MODULE 1 学以致用

Fill in the blanks with the proper English words given below.

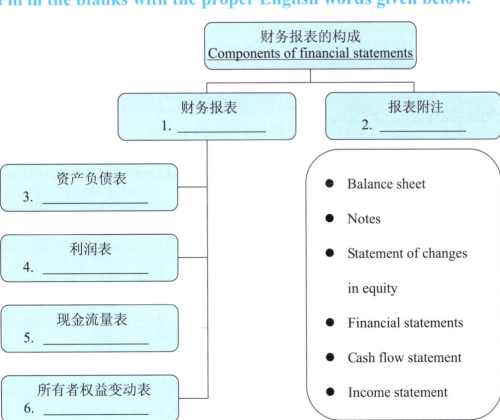

MODULE 2 手不释卷

A. Read the following information about financial statements.

1. Financial Statements

A financial statement is a formal record of an economic entity's financial activities. The purpose of a financial statement is to provide information about the financial position, financial performance, and cash flows of an economic entity, which is useful to a wide range of users in making proper economic decisions.

2. Contents of Financial Statements

To meet that objective, financial statements should provide information about an economic entity's assets, liabilities, equity, incomes and expenses (including gains and losses), contributions by and distributions to owners, cash flows, and other information in the notes.

A complete set of financial statements should include:

- ◇ a statement of financial position (balance sheet) at the end of the period;
- ◇ an income statement for the period and statement of cash flows for the period;
- ◇ a statement of changes in equity for the period;
- ◇ notes, including a summary of accounting policies and other explanatory notes.

3. Users of Financial Statements

The users of financial statements include the shareholders, management, employees, creditors, government, and other public bodies such as the trade union and community.

B. Learn the new words and phrases in the above passage and try to make sentences with them.

New Words

entity	[ˈentiti]	n. 主体，实体，独立存在体
contribution	[ˌkɔntriˈbjuːʃn]	n. 捐助物，贡献
distribution	[ˌdistriˈbjuːʃn]	n. 分发，分配
complete	[kəmˈpliːt]	adj. 完整的，完全的
policy	[ˈpɔləsi]	n. 政策，方针

Useful Expressions and Knowledge

1. financial statements 财务报表

财务报表亦称会计报表，有些英文材料用accounting statements 表示财务报表。在英国，人们常用financial accounts 来表示财务报表。

2. prepare financial statements 编制财务报表

一提到"编制"这个词，很多朋友会想到英文中的formation，而prepare 一般表示"准备、筹备"的意思。但英文里，人们习惯用prepare来表示"编制报表"中的"编制"一词。

3. financial position 财务状况

企业财务状况是企业在某一特定日期资产(assets)、负债(liabilities)及所有者/股东权益(owners'/ shareholders' equity)的情况。我们通常认为资产负债表(balance sheet)是表示财务状况的报表。在美国等国家/地区，人们也将资产负债表称为statement of financial position(财务状况表)。

4. financial performance 财务业绩，经营成果

企业经营成果一般由收入、费用和利润来体现。因此，income statement(利润表)在有些国家/地区也被称为statement of financial performance(财务业绩表)。

5. economic decision 经济决策

6. trade union 工会

工会在英国被称为trade union，在美国被称为labor union。

7. a wide range of 广大的，广泛的

8. a set of 一套

BALANCE SHEET

GOALS 学习目标

- Understand the typical format of a simple balance sheet.
- Be able to draft a simple balance sheet.

MODULE 1 学以致用

Fill in the blanks with the proper words and expressions given below, and change the form if necessary.

> benefit   asset   liability   interest   resource   obligation

1. What _____(资源) can we use to make better investment decisions?
2. The owner has the residual _____(利益) in the assets of the enterprise after deducting all the liabilities.
3. What's the economic _____(益处) of this new project?
4. The accounting elements included in the balance sheet are _____(资产), _____(负债), and owners' equity.
5. To pay taxes is an _____(责任).

MODULE 2 手不释卷

A. Read the following information about balance sheet.

1. Balance Sheet

The balance sheet is also referred to as the statement of financial position, showing the financial position of a business at a point in time. The accounting elements included in the balance sheet are assets, liabilities, and owners' (or shareholders') equity.

2. Balance Sheet and Accounting Equation

The balance sheet is prepared using the concept of the accounting equation.

- ✧ Assets are listed on the left and added to arrive at total assets.
- ✧ Liabilities and owners' equity are listed on the right and added to arrive at total liabilities and owners' equity.
- ✧ Exhibit 5-1 shows that total assets should be equal to the combined total liabilities and owners' equity; that is, the accounting equation must keep balance, which is how balance sheet got its name.

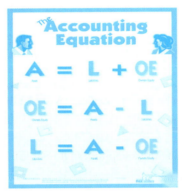

Exhibit 5-1　Accounting Equation

3. Disclosure of Assets, Liabilities, and Owners' Equity in the Balance Sheet

1) Assets (Shown in Exhibit 5-2)

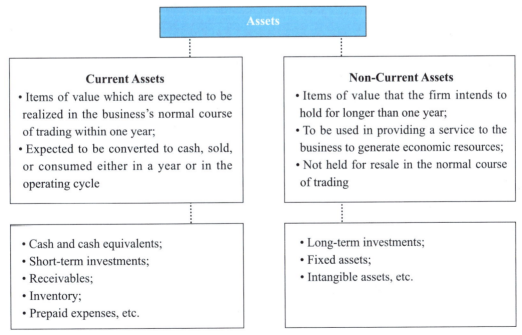

Exhibit 5-2　Classification of Assets

2) Liabilities (Shown in Exhibit 5-3)

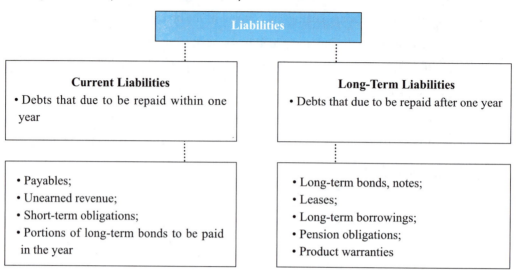

Exhibit 5-3   Classification of Liabilities

3) Owners' (Shareholders') Equity

Owners' equity normally includes capital (share value), capital (share) reserve, surplus reserves, and retained profit, etc.

B. Learn the new words and phrases in the above passage and try to make sentences with them.

New Words

concept	['kɔnsept]	n. 概念，观念
list	[list]	vt. 列出，列入
equal	['iːkwəl]	adj. 相等的
balance	['bæləns]	n. 平衡，均衡

Useful Expressions and Knowledge

1. a point in time 某一时点；某一日期

2. refer to 指的是

3. be equal to 等于

E.g. A is equal to B; B is equal to C; hence, A is equal to C.

例如，A等于B，B等于C，因此，A等于C。

4. accounting equation 会计等式

C. Test your understanding.

1. Translate the following balance sheet.

Background: ABC Co., Ltd. is a client of Smith Accounting Firm. Susan has prepared a balance sheet as of Dec. 31, 2022 for ABC Co., Ltd. as requested (see Exhibit 5-4).

Direction: As one of ABC's new stockholders—Mr. Chen only speaks Chinese, Susan wants you to translate the English balance sheet in Exhibit 5-4 into Chinese for Mr. Chen. Please use the blank sheet in Exhibit 5-5.

Information:

ABC Co., Ltd.			
Balance Sheet as of Dec. 31, 2022 ($)			
Assets		**Liabilities & Owners' Equity**	
Current assets		Liabilities	
Cash on hand	56	*Current liabilities*	
Cash at bank	1 704	Accounts payable	500
Accounts receivable	1 840	Wages payable	290
Inventory	2 390	Short-term borrowings	300
Total current assets	5 990	Total current liabilities	1 090
Non-current assets		*Long-term liabilities*	
Fixed assets	7 000	Loan (due on May 31, 2025)	2 900
Less: Accumulated depreciation	(500)	Total long-term liabilities	2 900
Intangible assets	1 000	Total liabilities	3 990
Total non-current assets	7 500		
		Owners' Equity	
		Capital	8 000
		Retained earnings	1 500
		Total owners' equity	9 500
Total assets	**13 490**	**Total liabilities and owners' equity**	**13 490**

Exhibit 5-4 Balance Sheet of ABC Co., Ltd.

1. _____			
Assets		**Liabilities & Owners' Equity**	
2. _____		Liabilities	
3. _____	56	13. _____	
4. _____	1 704	14. _____	500
5. _____	1 840	15. _____	290
6. _____	2 390	16. _____	300
7. _____	5 990	17. _____	1 090
8. _____		18. _____	
9. _____	7 000	19. _____	2 900
10. _____	(500)	20. _____	2 900
10. _____	1 000	Total liabilities	3 990
12. _____	7 500		
		Owners' Equity	
		21. _____	8 000
		22. _____	1 500
		Total owners' equity	9 500
Total assets	**13 490**	**Total liabilities and owners' equity**	**13 490**

Exhibit 5-5 Blank Balance Sheet of ABC Co., Ltd.

2. Try to prepare a balance sheet.

Background: Mr. Toney is a client of Smith Accounting Firm. He owns a shop named Toney Video Hire Shop. The relevant data about the shop's assets and liabilities as of Dec. 31, 2022 is given below.

Direction: Susan wants you to prepare the balance sheet for Toney Video Hire Shop as of Dec. 31, 2022.

Information: Stock of videos ($8 000); borrowing from National Bank ($3 500, due in Aug. 2024); cash at bank ($4 500); accounts receivable ($100); video equipment ($2 900); video equipment accumulated depreciation ($200); borrowing from Green ($400, due in Jun. 2023); accounts payable ($500).

MODULE 3 博学多才

Look at Exhibit 5-6, read the balance sheet of Microsoft Corp. from year 2006 to 2010, and make brief comments.

Microsoft Corp.

Statement of Financial Position($)

Period Ending	FY2010	FY2009	FY2008	FY2007	FY2006
Assets					
Cash and short-term investments	37.38 B	31.91 B	24.12 B	23.41 B	34.16 B
Net receivables	13.01 B	11.19 B	13.59 B	11.34 B	9.32 B
Total inventory	740.00 M	717.00 M	985.00 M	1.13 B	1.48 B
Progress payments & others	0.00	0.00	0.00	0.00	0.00
Prepaid expenses	—	—	—	—	—
Other current assets	4.54 B	5.46 B	4.55 B	4.29 B	4.06 B
Current assets total	55.68 B	49.28 B	43.24 B	40.17 B	49.01 B
Long-term receivables	0.00	0.00	0.00	0.00	0.00
Assets					
Investment in unconsolidated subsidiaries	—	—	—	—	—
Other investments	7.75 B	4.93 B	6.59 B	10.12 B	9.23 B
Property, plant & equipment net	7.63 B	7.54 B	6.24 B	4.35 B	3.04 B

Exhibit 5-6 Balance Sheet of Microsoft Corp. from Year 2006 to 2010

(续表)

Period Ending	FY2010	FY2009	FY2008	FY2007	FY2006
Property, plant & equipment gross	16.26 B	15.08 B	12.54 B	9.37 B	7.22 B
Accumulated depreciation	8.63 B	7.55 B	6.30 B	5.02 B	4.18 B
Other assets	15.05 B	15.86 B	15.77 B	7.15 B	5.70 B
Deferred charges	—	—	—	—	—
Tangible other assets	1.50 B	1.60 B	1.69 B	1.51 B	1.30 B
Intangible other assets	13.55 B	14.26 B	14.08 B	5.64 B	4.40 B
Total assets	86.11 B	77.61 B	71.84 B	61.78 B	66.99 B
Liabilities					
Short-term debt & current portion of long-term debt	1.00 B	2.00 B	0.00	0.00	0.00
Accrued payroll	3.28 B	3.16 B	2.93 B	2.32 B	1.94 B
Income taxes payable	1.07 B	725.00 M	3.25 B	1.04 B	1.56 B
Dividends payable	1.16 B	1.16 B	1.01 B	938.00 M	906.00 M
Other current liabilities	15.61 B	16.67 B	18.66 B	16.20 B	15.13 B
Current liabilities total	26.15 B	27.03 B	29.89 B	23.75 B	22.44 B
Long-term debt	4.94 B	3.75 B	0.00	0.00	0.00
Provision for risks & charges	6.89 B	—	—	—	—
Deferred taxes	229.00 M	−279.00 M	−949.00 M	−1.39 B	−2.61 B
Deferred income	1.18 B	1.28 B	1.90 B	1.87 B	1.76 B
Deferred tax liability in untaxed reserves	—	—	—	—	—
Other liabilities	558.00 M	6.27 B	4.72 B	6.45 B	5.29 B
Total liabilities	39.94 B	38.05 B	35.56 B	30.68 B	26.88 B
Shareholders' Equity					
Non-equity reserves	0.00	0.00	0.00	0.00	0.00
Minority interest	0.00	0.00	0.00	0.00	0.00
Shareholders' Equity					
Preferred stock	0.00	0.00	0.00	0.00	0.00
Common equity	46.18 B	39.56 B	36.29 B	31.10 B	40.10 B
Common stock	62.86 B	62.38 B	62.85 B	60.56 B	59.00 B

Exhibit 5-6　Balance Sheet of Microsoft Corp. from Year 2006 to 2010 (Continued)

(续表)

Period Ending	FY2010	FY2009	FY2008	FY2007	FY2006
Capital surplus	—	—	—	—	—
Revaluation reserves	0.00	0.00	0.00	0.00	0.00
Other appropriated reserves	—	—	—	—	—
Unappropriated (free) reserves	—	—	—	—	—
Retained earnings	−17.74 B	−23.79 B	−27.70 B	−31.11 B	−20.13 B
Equity in untaxed reserves	—	—	—	—	—
ESOP guarantees	0.00	0.00	0.00	0.00	0.00
Unrealized foreign exchange gain (loss)	−176.00 M	30.00 M	270.00 M	149.00 M	64.00 M
Unrealized gain (loss) on marketable securities	1.23 B	939.00 M	870.00 M	1.50 B	1.16 B
Treasury stock	0.00	0.00	0.00	0.00	0.00
Total liabilities & shareholders' equity	86.11 B	77.61 B	71.84 B	61.78 B	66.99 B
Common shares outstanding	8.67 B	8.91 B	9.15 B	9.38 B	10.06 B

Exhibit 5-6　Balance Sheet of Microsoft Corp. from Year 2006 to 2010 (Continued)

LESSON 3

INCOME STATEMENT

GOALS 学习目标

- Understand the typical format of a simple income statement.
- Be able to draft a simple income statement.

MODULE 1 学以致用

Fill in the blanks with the proper words and expressions given below, and change the form if necessary.

record	property	expense	administration
loss	receive	gross	investment

1. What is the _____ weight(毛重) of this cargo?
2. He made a large _____ (投资) in the business enterprise.
3. Who is in charge of the _____ (行政管理) of your company?
4. That car is my _____ (财产), and you mustn't use it without my permission.
5. Some _____ (记录) of ancient civilization were discovered recently.
6. He charged his hotel bill to his _____ (费用) account.
7. She has _____ (收到) his present, but she will not accept it.
8. Their company suffered heavy _____ (损失) in business last year.

MODULE 2 手不释卷

A. Read the following information about income statement.

1. Income Statement

An income statement shows the financial performance of an enterprise over a period of time. The accounting elements included in the income statement are revenues, expenses, and profits or losses.

The income statement is prepared following the accrual basis accounting, which means that incomes (or expenses) are recorded in the income statement as they are earned (or incurred) regardless of whether cash has been received (or paid).

2. Disclosure of Items on the Income Statement

An income statement must include the following items: revenues, financial expenses, share of the profits or losses of associates and joint ventures, tax expenses, profits or losses for the period, etc.

3. Format of Income Statement

The income statement is split into two parts. The first part gives the gross profits and the second part shows the net profits.

B. Learn the new words and phrases in the above passage and try to make sentences with them.

New Words

enterprise	['entəpraiz]	n. 企[事]业单位；公司
regardless	[ri'gɑːdlis]	adv. 不管，不顾
revenue	['revənjuː]	n. 收入，收益
financial	[fai'nænʃl]	adj. 财政的，金融的
associate	[ə'səuʃieit]	n. 联营的企业或单位

Useful Expressions and Knowledge

1. accrual basis accounting 权责发生制
2. period of time 一段时间，一定期间
3. disclosure of 公开，披露
4. joint ventures 合资企业
5. account for 列入预算
6. split into 分成……

C. Test your understanding.

1. Translate the following important sentences.

(1) An income statement shows the financial performance of an enterprise over a period of time.

_____

(2) The income statement is prepared following the accrual basis accounting.

_____

(3) The income statement is split into two parts. The first part gives the gross profits and the second part shows the net profits.

_____

2. Try to understand the income statement.

Background: SME Co. is a client of Smith Accounting Firm. Susan has prepared an income statement as of Dec. 31, 2022 for SME Co. as requested (see Exhibit 5-7).

Direction: Susan wants you to translate the English income statement in Exhibit 5-7 into Chinese and use the blank sheet in Exhibit 5-8.

SME Co.	
Income statement as of Dec. 31, 2022 ($)	
Revenue	15 000
Less: Cost of goods sold	(6 000)
Gross profit	**9 000**
Sales expenses	(2 000)
General and administrative expenses	(3 000)
Financial expenses	(1 000)
	(6 000)
Profit before tax	3 000
Income tax expense	(900)
Profit for the year	**2 100**

Exhibit 5-7　Income Statement of SME Co.

SME Co.	
1._____ ($)	
2. _____	15 000
Less: 3. _____	(6 000)
4. _____	**9 000**
5. _____	(2 000)
6. _____	(3 000)
7. _____	(1 000)
8. _____	(6 000)
	3 000

Exhibit 5-8　Blank Income Statement of SME Co.

SME Co.	
1._____ ($)	
9. _____	(900)
10. _____	**2 100**

Exhibit 5-8　Blank Income Statement of SME Co. (Continued)

3. Try to prepare an income statement.

Background: Andy met a problem when preparing an income statement for BTR Co. BTR Co. completed its service at an agreed price of $5 000 on Jan. 31, but the client promised to pay the amount on Feb. 25. Andy doesn't know if he should include this payment in the income of Jan.

Direction: Can you help Andy solve this problem?

MODULE 3 博学多才

Look at Exhibit 5-9, read the income statement of Microsoft Corp. from year 2006 to 2010, and make brief comments.

Microsoft Corp.
Income Statement($)

Period Ending	FY2010	FY2009	FY2008	FY2007	FY2006
Net Income/Starting Line	11.62 B	11.00 B	17.41 B	22.21 B	20.83 B
Operating Activities					
Depreciation, depletion & amortization	10.01 B	10.62 B	11.49 B	10.28 B	9.16 B
Depreciation & depletion	10.01 B	10.62 B	11.49 B	10.28 B	9.16 B
Amortization of intangible assets	—	—	—	—	—
Deferred income taxes and investment tax crudity	—	—	—	—	—
Deferred income taxes	—	—	—	—	—
Income tax credit	−113.00 M	−65.00 M	0.00	0.00	0.00
Other cash flow	7.34 B	10.49 B	19.98 B	8.44 B	1.47 B
Funds from operations	31.20 B	29.42 B	47.60 B	41.55 B	33.24 B
Extraordinary items & discontinued operations	0.00	0.00	0.00	0.00	0.00
Funds from/for other operating activities	4.92 B	−5.00 B	1.01 B	4.41 B	−2.59 B
Incline (decline) in receivables	−126.00 M	3.27 B	−24.00 M	980.00 M	−2.15 B

Exhibit 5-9　Income Statement of Microsoft Corp. from Year 2006 to 2010

(续表)

Period Ending	FY2010	FY2009	FY2008	FY2007	FY2006
Incline (decline) in inventory	342.00 M	1.10 B	−719.00 M	−1.49 B	−1.78 B
Incline (decline) in accounts payable	805.00 M	−439.00 M	−1.08 B	469.00 M	−119.00 M
Incline (decline) in income taxes payable	0.00	0.00	0.00	0.00	0.00
Incline (decline) in other accruals	0.00	0.00	0.00	0.00	0.00
Incline (decline) in other assets or liabilities	3.90 B	−8.93 B	2.83 B	4.46 B	1.46 B
Net cash flow/operating activities	36.12 B	24.42 B	48.60 B	45.97 B	30.65 B
Capital Expenditures (Additions to Fixed Assets)					
Additions to other assets	0.00	0.00	0.00	0.00	0.00
Net assets from acquisitions	1.21 B	7.84 B	28.11 B	17.22 B	11.65 B
Incline (decline) in inventory	0.00	0.00	0.00	0.00	0.00
Decrease in investments	0.00	0.00	0.00	0.00	0.00
Disposal of fixed assets	10.27 B	16.46 B	21.38 B	11.21 B	10.67 B
Other uses—investing	−33.18 B	−42.40 B	18.16 B	48.54 B	33.77 B
Other sources—investing	35.22 B	44.47 B	195.00 M	11.57 B	9.02 B
Net cash flow—investing	−32.44 B	−42.38 B	40.90 B	72.42 B	51.40 B
Proceeds from stock options	0.00	0.00	2.96 B	0.00	0.00
Other proceeds from sale/issues of stock	0.00	623.00 M	12.01 B	0.00	0.00
Com/Pfd purchase, retired, converted, redeemed	1.26 B	0.00	1.25 B	12.32 B	8.55 B
Financing Activities					
Long-term borrowings	52.24 B	82.84 B	122.96 B	100.87 B	88.36 B
Incline or decline in short-term borrowings	−1.23 B	−26.12 B	−34.22 B	2.34 B	4.58 B
Reduction in long-term debt	100.15 B	88.80 B	69.05 B	49.83 B	49.35 B
Cash dividends paid total	4.79 B	8.99 B	12.41 B	11.49 B	10.42 B
Common dividends (cash)	4.79 B	8.99 B	12.41 B	11.49 B	10.42 B
Preferred dividends (cash)	0.00	0.00	0.00	0.00	0.00
Other sources—financing	0.00	131.00 M	3.64 B	0.00	0.00
Other uses—financing	−6.40 B	−3.07 B	3.63 B	−1.36 B	−1.39 B
Net cash flow—financing	−61.59 B	−43.51 B	24.64 B	28.21 B	23.23 B
Effect of exchange rate on cash	−333.00 M	795.00 M	—	—	—
Changes in cash and/or liquid items	—	—	—	—	—

Exhibit 5-9　Income Statement of Microsoft Corp. from Year 2006 to 2010 (Continued)

CASH FLOW STATEMENT

GOALS 学习目标

- Understand the typical format of a cash flow statement.
- Be able to classify different types of cash flows.

MODULE 1 学以致用

On the basis of the Chinese given below, fill in the blanks with the proper English words, and change the form if necessary.

outflow   convert   inventory   advertise   operating activities
investing activities   financing activities

1. They held a sale to reduce their _____(存货).

2. There was some _____(外流) from the Hong Kong dollar in October amid the local stock market correction.

3. Are lawyers allowed to _____(广告)?

4. Preferred stock or _____(可转换的) bonds or stock warrants can be _____(转换) into common stock.

MODULE 2 手不释卷

A. Read the following information about cash flow statement.

1. Cash Flow Statement

A cash flow statement reports an enterprise's cash inflows and outflows over a period of time classified by operating, investing, and financing activities. A sample cash flow statement is shown in Exhibit 5-10.

STEVEN Co., Ltd. Cash Flow Statement as of Dec. 31, 2022 ($)	
Cash flows from operating activities	
Cash receipts from customers	9 500
Cash paid to suppliers and employees	(2 000)
Cash generated from operations	7 500
Interest paid	(2 000)
Income taxes paid	(3 000)
Net cash flows from operating activities	2 500
Cash flows from investing activities	
Proceeds from the sale of equipment	7 500
Dividends received	3 000
Net cash flows from investing activities	10 500
Cash flows from financing activities	
Dividends paid	(2 500)
Net cash flows from financing activities	(2 500)
Net cash inflow (or outflow) in cash and cash equivalents	**10 500**
Cash and cash equivalents (at the beginning of the year)	1 000
Cash and cash equivalents (at the end of the year)	11 500

Exhibit 5-10 Cash Flow Statement of STEVEN Co., Ltd.

2. Cash and Cash Equivalents

The term cash flow mentioned in the cash flow statement includes inflows and outflows of cash and cash equivalents.

 1) Cash

Cash consists of cash on hand and demand deposits. It includes cash on hand, cash at bank, and other cash.

2) Cash Equivalents

Cash equivalents are short-term, highly liquid investments that are readily convertible to known amount of cash.

3. Classification of Cash Flows

The statement of cash flows shall report cash flows during the period classified by operating, investing, and financing activities.

1) Operating Activities

Cash flows from operating activities include cash received from customers and cash paid to suppliers and employees, etc. This could include purchasing raw materials and other inventories, advertising and shipping the product, etc. Cash flows arising from taxes on income are normally classified as operating activities.

2) Investing Activities

Investing activities include the acquisition and disposal of long-term assets and other investments not included in cash equivalents, such as cash inflows or outflows related to the construction of fixed assets and disposal of subsidiary companies.

3) Financing Activities

Financing activities are activities that result in changes in the size and composition of the contributed equity and borrowings of the entity.

B. Learn the new words and phrases in the above passage and try to make sentences with them.

New Words

operating	[ˈɔpəreitiŋ]	*adj.* 运行的；经营的
invest	[inˈvest]	*vt. & vi.* 投资
financing	[faiˈnænsiŋ]	*n.* 筹集资金，融资
equivalent	[iˈkwivələnt]	*n.* 同等物，等价物
purchase	[ˈpəːtʃəs]	*vt.* 购买
shipping	[ˈʃipiŋ]	*n.* (货物的)运输，运送
acquisition	[ˌækwiˈziʃn]	*n.* 获得，获得物
disposal	[disˈpəuzl]	*n.* 清除，处理

Useful Expressions and Knowledge

1. cash equivalents 现金等价物
2. demand deposit 活期存款

    demand deposit 一般翻译成活期存款，而 term deposit 是定期存款。对于 demand deposit，银行一般不支付利息。

3. classified by 按……分类
4. long-term assets 长期资产
5. raw materials 原材料
6. result in 引起，导致
7. operating activity 经营活动
8. investing activity 投资活动
9. financing activity 筹资活动

C. On the basis of IAS7, classify the following activities into:

A. operating activities   B. investing activities   C. financing activities

1. _____ Acquisition of other firms' debt
2. _____ Expenditure for purchase of other firms' equity instruments
3. _____ Dividends received on equity securities
4. _____ Payments to suppliers for goods and services
5. _____ Payments to employees
6. _____ Proceeds from issuing shares
7. _____ Interest received on loans
8. _____ Tax payments
9. _____ Interest payments
10. _____ Receipts from sale of plant and equipment
11. _____ Receipts for the sale of equity in a trading portfolio
12. _____ Expenditure for purchase of plant and equipment
13. _____ Receipts from the sale of goods or services
14. _____ Proceeds from issuing short-term or long-term debt
15. _____ Payments for repurchase of company shares
16. _____ Repayment of debt principal, including capital leases

MODULE 3 博学多才

Look at Exhibit 5-11, read the cash flow statement of GE Co. from year 2006 to 2010, and make brief comments.

General Electric Co.

Cash Flow Statement($)

Period Ending	FY2010	FY2009	FY2008	FY2007	FY2006
Net Income/Starting Line	6.56 B	2.72 B	−14.67 B	−2.72 B	−12.61 B
Operating Activities					
Depreciation, depletion & amortization	5.90 B	7.67 B	12.92 B	13.16 B	16.52 B
Depreciation & depletion	5.80 B	7.58 B	12.83 B	13.05 B	16.45 B
Amortization of intangible assets	97.00 M	86.00 M	99.00 M	106.00 M	66.00 M
Deferred income taxes and investment tax credit	1.62 B	1.66 B	1.77 B	1.99 B	2.04 B
Deferred income taxes	1.62 B	1.66 B	1.77 B	1.99 B	2.04 B
Income tax credit	0.00	0.00	0.00	0.00	0.00
Other cash flow	1.16 B	2.90 B	11.54 B	5.85 B	6.88 B
Funds from operations	13.66 B	12.54 B	11.74 B	10.77 B	8.28 B
Extraordinary items & discontinued operations	0.00	0.00	0.00	0.00	0.00
Funds from/for other operating activities	−2.18 B	2.94 B	−11.91 B	6.30 B	1.35 B
Incline (decline) in receivables	765.00 M	2.61 B	1.09 B	45.00 M	2.28 B
Incline (decline) in inventories	−903.00 M	2.20 B	−358.00 M	371.00 M	−695.00 M
Incline (decline) in accounts payable	−704.00 M	−2.83 B	−12.65 B	1.35 B	6.53 B
Incline (decline) in income taxes payable	—	—	—	—	—
Incline (decline) in other accruals	—	—	—	—	—
Incline (decline) in other assets or liabilities	−1.34 B	955.00 M	0.00	4.54 B	−6.77 B
Net cash flow/operating activities	11.48 B	15.48 B	−179.00 M	17.07 B	9.62 B
Capital Expenditures (Additions to Fixed Assets)					
Additions to other assets	0.00	0.00	0.00	0.00	0.00
Net assets from acquisitions	28.87 B	26.39 B	13.00 M	26.00 M	0.00
Incline (decline) in inventories	100.15 B	78.20 B	64.75 B	11.42 B	23.68 B

Exhibit 5-11   Cash Flow Statement of GE Co. from Year 2006 to 2010

(续表)

Period Ending	FY2010	FY2009	FY2008	FY2007	FY2006
Decrease in investments	101.08 B	74.34 B	62.05 B	18.66 B	18.46 B
Disposal of fixed assets	1.32 B	1.29 B	6.85 B	1.24 B	56.00 M
Other uses—investing	−37.63 B	−39.63 B	580.00 M	8.88 B	12.86 B
Other sources—investing	38.12 B	40.36 B	44.91 B	46.88 B	46.95 B
Net cash flow—investing	−6.91 B	−6.62 B	3.14 B	6.46 B	24.88 B
Proceeds from stock options	0.00	0.00	0.00	0.00	0.00
Other proceeds from sale/issues of stock	1.34 B	2.45 B	756.00 M	250.00 M	431.00 M
Com/Pfd purchase, retired, converted, redeemed	0.00	0.00	0.00	31.00 M	183.00 M
Financing Activities					
Long-term borrowings	30.82 B	45.99 B	42.16 B	33.11 B	58.26 B
Incline or decline in short-term borrowings	−1.75 B	−5.88 B	−5.12 B	919.00 M	−5.82 B
Reduction in long-term debt	47.62 B	61.82 B	46.30 B	39.43 B	36.60 B
Cash dividends paid total	0.00	0.00	0.00	0.00	468.00 M
Common dividends (cash)	0.00	0.00	0.00	0.00	468.00 M
Preferred dividends (cash)	0.00	0.00	0.00	0.00	0.00
Other sources—financing	100.00 M	0.00	0.00	0.00	0.00
Other uses—financing	−7.20 B	−3.57 B	−604.00 M	−62.00 M	−339.00 M
Net cash flow—financing	−24.42 B	−22.83 B	−9.10 B	−5.24 B	15.27 B
Effect of exchange rate on cash	−53.00 M	454.00 M	−808.00 M	1.01 B	464.00 M
Changes in cash and/or liquid items	—	—	—	—	—

Exhibit 5-11 Cash Flow Statement of GE Co. from Year 2006 to 2010 (Continued)

PROJECT 5

1. Background: The accounting data of Landlubber Real Estate as of Dec. 31, 2022 is listed in Exhibit 5-12.

Task: Prepare the balance sheet as of Dec. 31, 2022 for this company on the basis of its accounting data.

Transactions: On Dec. 31, 2022, Landlubber Real Estate had the following assets and liabilities, as shown in Exhibit 5-12.

Cash on hand	$300	Bank loan (due in Jun. 2023)	$4 000
Bank overdraft	$11 000	Stock of stationery	$300
Land and buildings	$90 000	Motor vehicles	$28 000
Accounts receivable	$17 000	Office equipment	$6 000
Mortgage loan	$44 000	Office furniture	$1 750
Accounts payable	$16 000		

Exhibit 5-12　Information of Assets and Liabilities

Direction and Relevant Table: Prepare the classified balance sheet (See Exhibit 5-13) as of Dec. 31, 2022.

Landlubber Real Estate Balance Sheet as of Dec. 31, 2022 ($)			
Assets		**Liabilities & owners' equity**	
Current assets		**Liabilities**	
Cash on hand	300	*Current liabilities*	
Accounts receivable	17 000		
Stock of stationery	300		
		Total current liabilities	
		Long-term liabilities	
Total current assets			
Non-current assets			
		Total long-term liabilities	
		Total liabilities	
		Owners' equity	
Total non-current assets			

Exhibit 5-13　Balance Sheet

(续表)

Landlubber Real Estate **Balance Sheet as of Dec. 31, 2022 ($)**			
Total assets		Total owners' equity Total liabilities and owners' equity	

Exhibit 5-13   Balance Sheet (Continued)

2. Background: Some accounting data of G. Kight Co. as of Jun. 30, 2022 is listed in Exhibit 5-14.

Tasks:

(1) Prepare the balance sheet as of Jun. 30, 2022 for G. Kight Co.

(2) Prepare the income statement as of Jun. 30, 2022 for G. Kight Co.

Transactions: On Jun. 30, 2022, G. Kight Co. had the following assets and liabilities, as shown in Exhibit 5-14.

Cash at bank	$4 000	Insurance expenses	$4 200
Fees earned	$52 000	Drawings, K Wyatt	$8 800
Wages	$21 000	Capital, K Wyatt	?
Accounts receivable	$7 500	Stock of stationery	$750
Accounts payable	$4 800	Stationery used	$250
Advertising	$2 200	Discount received	$150
Commission earned	$17 000	Discount allowed	$100
Land and buildings	$85 000	Motor vehicles	$18 550
Mortgage—land & buildings	$45 000		

Exhibit 5-14   Information of Assets and Liabilities

Directions and Relevant Tables:

(1) Prepare the balance sheet (see Exhibit 5-15) as of Jun. 30, 2022.

G. Kight Co. **Balance Sheet as of Jun. 30, 2022 ($)**			
Assets *Current assets* *Total current assets* *Non-current assets*		**Liabilities & Owners' Equity** **Liabilities** *Current liabilities* *Total current liabilities* *Long-term liabilities*	

Exhibit 5-15   Balance Sheet

(续表)

		G. Kight Co. Balance Sheet as of Jun. 30, 2022 ($)	
Total non-current assets **Total assets**		***Total long-term liabilities*** **Total liabilities** **Owners' Equity** **Total owners' equity** **Total liabilities and owners' equity**	

Exhibit 5-15   Balance Sheet (Continued)

(2) Prepare the income statement (see Exhibit 5-16) as of Jun. 30, 2022.

G. Kight Co. Income Statement as of Jun. 30, 2022($)	
Gross profit **Profit for the year**	

Exhibit 5-16   Income Statement

UNIT 6

INTERPRETATION OF FINANCIAL STATEMENTS

您好!
　　我是FM基金公司的George，我在为投资者们寻找具备潜力的目标公司。接下来让我们一起学习财务分析。

Goals 学习目标

- Understand the purposes and importance of interpreting financial statements in assessing a company's financial performance.
- Learn key financial ratios and metrics used in the interpretation of financial statements.
- Gain insights into the limitations of interpreting financial statements.

Guidance 学习指导

　　财务报表的作用是向利益相关者提供有用的财务信息，不同的使用者有着不同的信息需求。作为一个财务分析师，当你拿到企业的资产负债表和利润表时，如何从财务信息的维度评判企业的经营状况？这就涉及财务比率分析，通常包括流动性、盈利能力、营运能力和偿债能力等财务指标的分析。在进行初步分析后，财务分析师需要综合考虑行业环境、竞争情况及其他重要因素，以便更客观地理解和评估公司的财务状况和经营情况。

　　党的二十大报告指出："改革开放和社会主义现代化建设深入推进，书写了经济快速发展和社会长期稳定两大奇迹新篇章，我国发展具备了更为坚实的物质基础、更为完善的制度保证，实现中华民族伟大复兴进入了不可逆转的历史进程。"可见，当前形势为财务分析工作提供了良好的大环境。

LESSON 1

INTRODUCTION TO FINANCIAL STATEMENT INTERPRETATION

GOALS 学习目标

- Understand the importance of financial statement interpretation.
- Understand the role of interpretation in decision-making processes.

MODULE 1 学以致用

1. Financial statement interpretation helps in _____(识别趋势).

2. Financial statement interpretation plays a crucial role in _____(决策支持).

3. Financial statement interpretation is essential for _____(法规遵循).

4. Effective financial statement interpretation promotes communication and _____(透明性).

MODULE 2 手不释卷

A. Read the following information about financial statement interpretation.

1. Importance of Financial Statement Interpretation

1) Basic Concepts

Financial statement interpretation allows stakeholders to evaluate a company's financial performance by analyzing key indicators such as profitability, liquidity, solvency, and operational efficiency. This assessment helps in understanding the company's financial health and its ability to generate profits and cash flows.

2) Purposes of Financial Statement Interpretation

◇ To Understand Financial Position

Interpreting financial statements helps in assessing a company's financial position by analyzing its assets, liabilities, and equity. This evaluation provides insights into the company's ability to meet its short-term and long-term obligations, as well as its overall financial stability.

◆ To Identify Trends

Financial statement interpretation helps in identifying trends and patterns in a company's financial data over time. It allows stakeholders to identify strengths and weaknesses in the company's financial performance, highlighting areas of improvement or concern.

◆ For Decision-Making Support

Financial statement interpretation plays a crucial role in decision-making processes. It provides valuable insights and information that support investment decisions, such as evaluating potential investments and assessing the risk-return tradeoff. It also assists lenders in determining the creditworthiness of a borrower and aids management in strategic planning and decision-making.

◆ For Compliance and Reporting

Financial statement interpretation is essential for regulatory compliance and reporting purposes. It ensures that financial statements adhere to accounting standards and regulatory requirements, providing accurate and reliable information to stakeholders.

◆ For Communication and Transparency

Effective financial statement interpretation promotes communication and transparency between a company and its stakeholders. It enables clear and meaningful communication of financial information, fostering trust and confidence among investors, lenders, and other interested parties.

2. Role of Interpretation in Decision-Making Processes for Different Users

1) Evaluating Investment Opportunities

Interpreting financial statements helps investors and financial analysts assess investment opportunities. By analyzing key financial indicators and trends, stakeholders can make informed decisions about investing in a company's stocks, bonds, or other financial instruments.

2) Supporting Strategic Planning

Financial statement interpretation provides valuable insights for managers to make strategic plans. It helps the management identify strengths and weaknesses in the company's financial position, assess the feasibility of proposed strategies, and make informed decisions regarding resource allocation, expansion plans, mergers and acquisitions, and other strategic initiatives.

3) Facilitating Budgeting and Forecasting

Interpreting financial statements supports accountants in the budgeting and forecasting processes. By analyzing the historical financial data, stakeholders can identify trends, patterns, and relationships that aid in making accurate revenue and expense projections, setting realistic financial targets, and making budgetary decisions.

4) Assisting Credit Decisions

Financial statement interpretation is vital for banks in assessing the creditworthiness of a company. Lenders and creditors analyze a company's financial statements to evaluate its ability to repay loans, manage debt levels, and meet financial obligations. This information helps lenders make informed credit decisions, such as determining loan terms, interest rates, and credit limits.

5) Monitoring Performance

Financial statement interpretation enables stakeholders to monitor and evaluate a company's ongoing performance. By comparing actual financial results with projected targets, stakeholders can identify deviations, assess performance against industry benchmarks, and take necessary corrective actions to ensure financial goals can be achieved.

B. Learn the new words and phrases in the above passage and try to make sentences with them.

New Words

benchmark	[ˈbentʃmɑːrk]	n. 基准，标杆
compliance	[kəmˈplaɪəns]	n. 合规性，遵守
creditworthiness	[ˈkredɪtˌwɜːrðinəs]	n. 信用价值，信用能力
facilitate	[fəˈsɪlɪteɪt]	v. 促进，帮助
feasibility	[ˌfiːzəˈbɪləti]	n. 可行性
improvement	[ɪmˈpruːvmənt]	n. 改进，提升
interpretation	[ɪnˌtɜːrprɪˈteɪʃn]	n. 解释，解读
obligation	[ˌɑːblɪˈɡeɪʃn]	n. 义务，责任
projection	[prəˈdʒekʃn]	n. 预测，预测数据
stakeholder	[ˈsteɪkhəʊldər]	n. 利益相关者
transparency	[trænsˈpærənsi]	n. 透明度

Useful Expressions and Knowledge

1. expansion plans 扩张计划
2. financial instruments 金融工具
3. financial performance 财务绩效
4. financial position 财务状况
5. mergers and acquisitions 兼并与收购
6. resource allocation 资源配置
7. risk-return tradeoff 风险与回报的权衡
8. strategic initiatives 战略举措

C. Test your understanding.

Match the words listed in the following box with the relevant descriptions listed below.

A. Investors
B. Lenders
C. Management
D. Suppliers
E. Regulatory authorities
F. Employees
G. Customers

(1) While they may not have direct access to financial statements, they indirectly rely on financial information to assess the company's reliability and long-term viability. They may consider factors such as pricing stability, product quality, and customer satisfaction, which are influenced by the company's financial performance and stability. (　　)

(2) They are interested in the financial stability and growth potential of the company. They may look at information related to employee benefits, such as pension plans and profit-sharing programs, as well as financial performance indicators that reflect the company's ability to provide job security and career opportunities. (　　)

(3) They require financial information to ensure compliance with accounting standards and regulations. They focus on accurate and transparent financial reporting. Therefore, they may require detailed financial statements, disclosures, and adherence to specific accounting principles. (　　)

(4) They often assess a company's financial health before extending credit or entering into

business partnerships. They rely on information related to liquidity, payment history, and profitability. Key financial indicators for suppliers include the current ratio, quick ratio, and accounts payable turnover ratio. (   )

(5) They needs comprehensive financial information to make strategic decisions and monitor the company's performance. They require financial statements, including the income statement, balance sheet, and cash flow statement, to assess profitability, liquidity, and cash flow. Ratios such as gross profit margin, operating profit margin, and cash conversion cycle help the management identify areas of improvement and measure operational efficiency. (   )

(6) They focus on the company's ability to repay both short-term and long-term debts. They need information on liquidity, cash flow, and debt ratios, such as the debt-to-equity ratio and interest coverage ratio. This helps them evaluate the company's creditworthiness and repayment capacity. (   )

(7) They are primarily interested in the profitability and financial performance of a company. They need information such as net profit, earnings per share (EPS), and return on investment (ROI) to assess the company's financial health and make informed investment decisions. (   )

MODULE 3 博学多才

A. Help your understanding.

用于财务报表分析的技术与工具

　　财务报表提供了关于企业资产、负债、所有者权益、收入、费用及利润的财务信息。对于股东、投资者和其他利益相关者来说，这些信息可能并不容易理解。因此，财务会计和分析师通常采用各种技术来分析和解释财务报表，使得财务信息更容易被理解和比较。财务报表分析技术主要有以下三类。

　　1) 横向分析

　　该分析方法用于企业之间的比较。例如，将A公司在某一会计期间的财务信息与行业平均水平或其他相似企业的财务信息进行比较。如果A公司本年度的利润率为15%，我们无法据此得出A公司强于市场平均水平的结论，因此需要进一步分析同一期间内目标企业所处行业的平均利润率，假设行业平均利润率为12%，那么我们可以得出结论：A公司利润率高于行业平均水平。

2) 时间序列分析

这种方法用于企业自身财务数据的比较，即比较同一企业不同年份的财务报表，比如通过比较当年利润和去年利润，分析相关趋势。

3) 横向和时间序列综合分析

这种分析旨在比较两个或多个企业在特定会计期间的财务特征，能够结合两种分析方法的优点。

FINANCIAL RATIO ANALYSIS

GOALS 学习目标

- Understand the key financial ratios and metrics used in the interpretation of financial statements.
- Understand the limitations of interpreting financial statements.

MODULE 1 学以致用

1. _____(流动能力比率) are financial metrics that assess a company's ability to meet its short-term obligations and measure its liquidity position.

2. _____(盈利能力比率) are important financial metrics that help assess a company's ability to generate profits and measure its overall financial performance.

3. _____(效率比率) play a crucial role in assessing a company's operational efficiency and the effectiveness of its working capital management.

4. _____(杠杆比率) are essential in evaluating a company's capital structure and its ability to meet its financial obligations.

MODULE 2 手不释卷

A. Read the following information about financial ratio analysis.

1. Introduction to Financial Ratios (Shown in Exhibit 6-1)

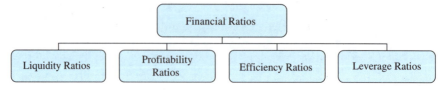

Exhibit 6-1　Classification of Financial Ratios

Financial ratios are quantitative metrics used to analyze and assess the financial health and performance of a company. They provide valuable insights into various aspects of a company's profitability, efficiency, liquidity, and solvency. Understanding and interpreting financial ratios is essential for investors, analysts, and stakeholders to make informed decisions and evaluate the overall financial performance of a company.

Financial ratios allow for meaningful comparisons between different companies, industries, or time periods. They provide a standardized way of measuring and benchmarking key financial indicators, enabling stakeholders to identify trends, strengths, and weaknesses.

The significance of financial ratios lies in their ability to provide a snapshot of a company's financial position and performance. For example, liquidity ratios such as the current ratio and the quick ratio indicate a company's ability to meet short-term obligations. Profitability ratios such as return on capital employed (ROCE) and return on equity (ROE) measure a company's ability to generate profits from its assets and equity investments. Efficiency ratios such as inventory turnover period and receivables collection period evaluate how efficiently a company manages its assets and collects its receivables. Leverage ratios such as debt-to-equity ratio and interest coverage ratio assess a company's financial leverage and ability to cover its interest payments.

2. Liquidity Ratios (Shown in Exhibit 6-2)

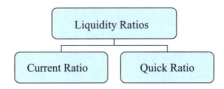

Exhibit 6-2　Classification of Liquidity Ratios

Liquidity ratios are financial metrics that assess a company's ability to meet its short-term obligations and measure its liquidity position. Two commonly used liquidity ratios are the current ratio and the quick ratio.

1) Current Ratio

$$\text{Current Ratio} = \frac{\text{Current Assets}}{\text{Current Liabilities}}$$

The current ratio is a liquidity ratio that compares a company's current assets to its current liabilities. It is calculated by dividing current assets by current liabilities. The current assets include cash, accounts receivable, inventory, and other assets that are expected to be converted into cash within one year, while current liabilities include accounts payable, short-term debt, and other obligations due within one year. The current ratio measures the company's ability to cover its short-term obligations with its current assets.

2) Quick Ratio

$$\text{Quick Ratio} = \frac{\text{Current Assets} - \text{Inventory}}{\text{Current Liabilities}}$$

The quick ratio, also known as the acid-test ratio, is a more stringent measure of liquidity. It excludes inventory from current assets since inventory may not be easily converted into cash in a short period. The quick ratio is calculated by dividing the sum of cash, accounts receivable, and short-term investments (or current assets minus inventory) by current liabilities. The quick ratio provides a more conservative assessment of a company's ability to meet its short-term obligations. It measures the company's ability to meet its immediate liabilities without relying on the sale of inventory. A higher quick ratio indicates a stronger liquidity position and a greater ability to meet short-term obligations.

3) Interpretation of Liquidity Ratios

Interpretation of liquidity ratios, such as the current ratio and the quick ratio, is crucial for understanding a company's ability to meet its short-term obligations and manage its liquidity position effectively.

The current ratio is an important liquidity ratio that measures a company's ability to cover its short-term liabilities with its current assets. A current ratio greater than 1 indicates that the company has more current assets than current liabilities, suggesting a favorable liquidity position. However, an excessively high current ratio may indicate an inefficient use of assets, such as excessive cash holdings or slow inventory turnover. On the other hand, a current ratio less than 1 may raise concerns about the company's ability to meet its short-term obligations. The interpretation of the current ratio depends on the industry norms and the specific circumstances of the company.

The quick ratio, also known as the acid-test ratio, provides a more conservative measure of liquidity by excluding inventory from current assets. This ratio focuses on the company's ability to meet its immediate obligations without relying on the sale of inventory. A higher quick ratio is generally considered more favorable, as it indicates a stronger ability to cover short-term liabilities. However, an excessively high quick ratio may imply that the company is overly cautious in managing its cash and may not be utilizing its assets efficiently.

When interpreting liquidity ratios, one must consider industry benchmarks and compare the company's ratios with its peers. Different industries have varying liquidity requirements, and what may be considered adequate in one industry might be considered low in another. Additionally, trend analysis is valuable in understanding the company's liquidity position over time. Comparing liquidity ratios from different periods allows for the identification of any significant changes or trends that may impact the company's ability to meet its short-term obligations.

It is important to note that liquidity ratios should not be analyzed in isolation but should be considered alongside other financial ratios and qualitative factors. Liquidity analysis should be complemented with a comprehensive examination of the company's cash flow statement, working capital management, debt structure, and overall financial health. Understanding the reasons behind changes in liquidity ratios and their implications on the company's financial position is crucial for making informed decisions.

3. Profitability Ratios (Shown in Exhibit 6-3)

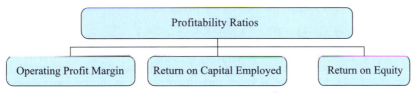

Exhibit 6-3　Classification of Profitability Ratios

Profitability ratios are important financial metrics that help assess a company's ability to generate profits and measure its overall financial performance. Three key profitability ratios commonly used by investors, analysts, and management are operating profit margin, return on capital employed (ROCE), and return on equity (ROE).

1) Operating Profit Margin

$$\text{Operating Profit Margin} = \frac{\text{Profit Before Interest and Taxation}}{\text{Revenue}} * 100\%$$

Operating profit margin, also known as operating margin, is a profitability ratio that measures the company's operating efficiency and profitability. It is calculated by dividing the profit before interest and taxation (PBIT) by the revenue and multiplying by 100%. Operating profit margin indicates the percentage of revenue that is converted into operating profit. A higher operating profit margin suggests better cost management and operational efficiency.

2) Return on Capital Employed

$$\text{ROCE} = \frac{\text{Profit Before Interest and Taxation}}{\text{Capital Employed}} * 100\%$$

Return on capital employed (ROCE) is a profitability ratio that measures how effectively a company utilizes its capital to generate profits. It is calculated by dividing the profit before interest and taxation (PBIT) by the capital employed (total assets minus current liabilities) and multiplying by 100%. ROCE indicates the return generated on the company's capital investment. A higher ROCE indicates efficient capital utilization and higher profitability relative to the capital employed.

3) Return on Equity

$$\text{Return on Equity} = \frac{\text{Net Income}}{\text{Average Shareholders' Equity}}$$

Return on equity (ROE) is a profitability ratio that measures the return generated on shareholders' equity. It is calculated by dividing the net income by the average shareholders' equity. ROE indicates the profitability of shareholders' investments in the company. A higher ROE suggests better profitability and effective management of shareholders' investments.

4) Interpretation of Profitability Ratios

The operating profit margin measures the profitability of a company's core operations by expressing the operating profit as a percentage of net sales. A higher operating profit margin indicates that the company is generating more profit from each dollar of sales, which is generally favorable. However, it is important to compare the operating profit margin with industry benchmarks and historical performance to gain a better understanding of the company's profitability. A declining or low operating profit margin may indicate issues such as increased costs, pricing pressures, or inefficiencies in operations that require further investigation.

Return on capital employed (ROCE) measures the efficiency with which a company utilizes its capital to generate profits. ROCE reflects the company's ability to generate returns on its investments and indicates the effectiveness of its capital allocation. A higher ROCE suggests that the company is utilizing its capital efficiently and generating satisfactory returns. However, the interpretation of ROCE should consider industry norms, as different industries may have varying capital requirements and profitability expectations.

Return on equity (ROE) measures the profitability of a company from the perspective of its shareholders. ROE indicates the return earned on the shareholders' investment and is a measure of the company's ability to generate profits with the funds provided by shareholders. A higher ROE indicates that the company is generating better returns for its shareholders. However, it is important to consider the underlying factors influencing ROE, such as debt levels and leverage, as excessive borrowing can artificially inflate ROE.

4. Efficiency Ratios (Shown in Exhibit 6-4)

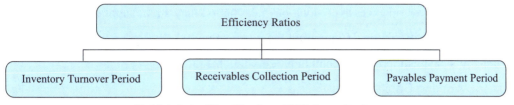

Exhibit 6-4   Classification of Efficiency Ratios

Efficiency ratios play a crucial role in assessing a company's operational efficiency and the effectiveness of its working capital management. Key efficiency ratios include the inventory turnover period (days), receivables collection period (days), payables payment period (days), and the working capital cycle.

1) Inventory Turnover Period

$$\text{Inventory Turnover Period} = \frac{\text{Inventory}}{\text{Cost of Sales}} * 365 \text{ Days}$$

The inventory turnover period measures the number of days it takes for a company to sell its inventory. A lower inventory turnover period indicates efficient inventory management and a faster conversion of inventory into sales. However, an extremely low turnover period may suggest inventory stockouts or ineffective sales strategies. It is important to compare the inventory turnover period with industry benchmarks and historical data to evaluate the company's inventory management efficiency.

2) Receivables Collection Period

$$\text{Receivables Collection Period} = \frac{\text{Trade Receivables}}{\text{Revenue}} * 365 \text{ Days}$$

The receivables collection period measures the average number of days it takes for a company to collect its accounts receivable. A shorter collection period indicates effective credit management and prompt collection of customer payments. Conversely, a longer collection period may indicate issues such as lenient credit policies or difficulties in collecting payments. It is essential to analyze the collection period in relation to industry norms and the company's credit terms and policies.

3) Payables Payment Period

$$\text{Payables Payment Period} = \frac{\text{Trade Payables}}{\text{Cost of Sales}} * 365 \text{ Days}$$

The payables payment period measures the average number of days it takes for a company to pay its suppliers or settle its payables. A longer payment period may indicate favorable terms negotiated with suppliers, allowing the company to maintain a strong cash position. However, an excessively long payment period may strain supplier relationships or signal cash flow difficulties. Comparing the payment period with industry averages and the company's payment terms is crucial in interpreting this ratio.

4) Working Capital Cycle

$$\text{Working Capital Cycle} = \text{Inventory Days} + \text{Receivable Days} - \text{Payable Days}$$

The working capital cycle represents the time it takes for a company to convert its investments in inventory and accounts receivable into cash by considering the inventory days, receivable days, and payable days. A shorter working capital cycle suggests efficient management of working capital and faster cash conversion. It signifies the company's ability to optimize its operational processes and generate cash inflows. Analyzing the working capital cycle helps identify areas where improvements can be made to enhance cash flow and operational efficiency.

5. Leverage Ratios (Shown in Exhibit 6-5)

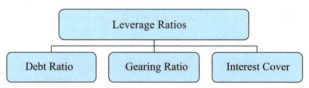

Exhibit 6-5   Classification of Leverage Ratios

Leverage ratios are essential in evaluating a company's capital structure and its ability to meet its financial obligations, and they are used to evaluate solvency. Key leverage ratios include debt ratio, gearing ratio, and interest cover ratio.

1) Debt Ratio

$$\text{Debt Ratio} = \frac{\text{Total Debts}}{\text{Total Assets}}$$

The debt ratio is the ratio of a company's total debts to its total assets. It measures the percentage of a company's assets financed by debts, indicating the level of financial leverage in the company's capital structure.

2) Gearing Ratio

$$\text{Gearing Ratio} = \frac{\text{Total Debts}}{\text{Total Equities}}$$

The gearing ratio assesses the proportion of a company's capital structure that is funded by debts compared to equities. It is calculated by dividing total debts by total equities. A higher gearing ratio indicates a higher reliance on debt financing, which can amplify both potential returns and risks. It is important to compare the gearing ratio with industry peers and historical data to understand the company's leverage position and its ability to manage debt obligations.

3) Interest Cover Ratio

$$\text{Interest Cover Ratio} = \frac{\text{Operating Profit}}{\text{Interest Expenses}}$$

The interest cover ratio assesses a company's ability to meet its interest payment obligations on its debt. It measures the number of times a company's operating profit can cover its interest expenses. A higher interest cover ratio indicates a better ability to meet interest payments and suggests a lower risk of default. This ratio is particularly important for companies with significant debt obligations, as a low interest cover ratio may indicate financial distress and an increased risk of default.

6. Limitations of Financial Statement Interpretation

Financial statement interpretation is a valuable tool for analyzing a company's financial performance and making informed decisions. However, it is important to recognize and understand the limitations associated with financial statement interpretation.

One limitation is the reliance on historical data. Financial statements provide information about the past performance of a company, but they may not reflect the current or future circumstances. Economic conditions, industry trends, and internal changes within the company can all impact its financial position and performance. Therefore, it is crucial to supplement financial statement analysis with other sources of information, such as market research and industry analysis, to gain a more comprehensive understanding of the company's current and future prospects.

Another limitation is the potential for manipulation and bias in financial reporting. While financial statements are subject to auditing and regulatory standards, there is still a risk of intentional or unintentional misrepresentation of financial information. Companies may employ accounting techniques or practices that obscure the true financial position, making it challenging to accurately interpret the statements. It is essential to exercise professional skepticism and conduct a thorough analysis of the financial statements, considering potential red flags or inconsistencies.

Additionally, financial statements may not capture all relevant information. They primarily focus on quantitative data, such as monetary values and financial ratios. However, qualitative factors, such as management capabilities, brand reputation, and market dynamics, can significantly impact a company's performance and prospects. These qualitative factors are not explicitly captured in financial statements and require additional research and analysis to assess their impact on the company's financial position.

Lastly, financial statement interpretation relies on assumptions and estimates. In some cases, companies may need to make judgments or estimates when preparing financial statements, such as the valuation of assets or the recognition of contingent liabilities. These estimates can be subjective and may vary among different companies or industry practices. Therefore, it is important to consider the inherent uncertainties and potential variability in financial statement data when interpreting the results.

To mitigate these limitations, financial analysts and decision-makers should adopt a holistic approach to analysis, incorporating both quantitative and qualitative factors. They should also consider the limitations and potential biases associated with financial statements and seek additional sources of information to supplement their analysis. Regular monitoring and reassessment of financial performance and market conditions are crucial to ensure that decisions are based on the most up-to-date and reliable information available.

B. Learn the new words and phrases in the above passage and try to make sentences with them.

New Words

acid-test	['æsɪd͵test]	n. 酸性测算
amplify	['æmplɪ͵faɪ]	v. 放大，增强
conservative	[kən'sɜrvətɪv]	adj. 保守的，谨慎的
default	[dɪ'fɔlt]	n. 违约，拖欠
inconsistency	[͵ɪnkən'sɪstənsi]	n. 不一致，矛盾
inflate	[ɪn'fleɪt]	v. 膨胀，通货膨胀
manipulation	[mə͵nɪpjʊ'leɪʃn]	n. 操纵，篡改
misrepresentation	[͵mɪs͵reprɪzen'teɪʃn]	n. 误传，歪曲
mitigate	['mɪtɪ͵geɪt]	v. 缓解，减轻
snapshot	['snæpˌʃɑt]	n. 概览
solvency	['sɑlvənsi]	n. 偿债能力，偿付能力
stockout	['stɑk͵aʊt]	n. 缺货，断货

Useful Expressions and Knowledge

1. contingent liabilities 或有负债
2. current ratio 流动比率
3. debt ratio 资产负债率
4. gearing ratio 杠杆比率
5. interest cover ratio 利息保障倍数
6. inventory turnover period 存货周转周期
7. operating profit margin 营业利润率
8. payables payment period 应付款项支付周期
9. profit before interest and taxation 息税前利润
10. quick ratio 速动比率
11. receivables collection period 应收款项回收周期
12. return on capital employed 资本回报率
13. return on equity 权益回报率
14. working capital cycle 营运资本周转周期

C. Test your understanding.

Background: Exhibit 6-6 and Exhibit 6-7 show the statement of profit or loss and the statement of financial position respectively for Mid Journey for the years as of Dec. 31, 2021 and Dec. 31, 2022.

Mid Journey Statement of Profit or Loss as of Dec. 31, 2021 and Dec. 31, 2022 ($)		
(*Amounts in thousands*)	2021	2022
Sales revenue	840	830
Cost of sales	554	591
Gross profit	286	239
Selling, distribution, and administration expenses	186	182
Profit before interest	100	57
Interest	6	8
Profit before tax	94	49
Tax (standard rate 50%)	45	23
Profit for the year	49	26

Exhibit 6-6 Statement of Profit or Loss

Mid Journey Statement of Financial Position as of Dec. 31, 2021 and Dec. 31, 2022 ($)		
(*Amounts in thousands*)	2021	2022
Non-current assets		
Intangible assets	36	32
Tangible assets at net book value	176	222
Total non-current assets	212	254
Current assets		
Inventory	237	265
Receivables	105	132
Bank	52	13
Total current assets	394	410
Total assets	606	664
Equity		
Share capital (ordinary 50c shares)	100	100
Retained earnings	299	348
Total equity	399	448
Non-current liabilities		
Long-term loans	74	94
Current liabilities		
Payables	133	122
Total liabilities	207	216
Total equity and liabilities	606	664

Exhibit 6-7   Statement of Financial Position

Direction: Compute and explain efficiency ratios and leverage ratios.

MODULE 3 博学多才

Visit the relevant websites and write down some useful information you've learnt from it in English.

1. https://www.investopedia.com/terms/d/dupontanalysis.asp

    推荐理由：杜邦分析(DuPont Analysis)是一种财务分析模型，将权益回报率

(ROE)的计算公式拆分、变形后，将它与其他财务指标相关联，提供了一个更全面的财务评估框架。

2. https://kfknowledgebank.kaplan.co.uk/the-balanced-scorecard-

推荐理由：传统的财务比率分析主要关注财务信息的分析，如利润率和权益回报率等，忽视了非财务信息的分析。平衡记分卡(Balanced Scorecard)提供了更全面的视角，其中包含财务指标和非财务指标，通过将财务、客户、内部流程和学习与成长这四个关键维度结合起来，帮助信息使用者更全面地评估目标企业的情况。

UNIT 7

ACCOUNTING IN A DIGITAL WORLD

Goals 学习目标

- Have general ideas of the digital world.
- Understand the basic concepts of digital technologies and their impacts on finance function.

Guidance 学习指导

党的二十大报告指出:"加快发展数字经济,促进数字经济和实体经济深度融合,打造具有国际竞争力的数字产业集群。"随着科技的迅速发展,数字化技术正在以前所未有的速度改变着世界。数字化技术正在改变人们的生活方式,同时对许多行业产生了颠覆性的影响。为适应数字化时代,许多大型企业率先进行数字化转型以保持竞争力。在此背景下,财会人员也被卷入了数字化转型的浪潮中,财务职能不再像过去那样仅仅涉及记账和编制报表等任务,在数字化时代,财会专业人员需要利用各种数字工具和技术,为信息使用者提供数据信息,分析问题,以及支持决策。

LESSON 1

THE DIGITAL WORLD AND BUSINESS ENVIRONMENT

GOALS 学习目标

- Understand the industrial revolutions, especially the Fourth Industrial Revolution.
- Understand the definition of the digital world and what significant changes have occurred in the business environment.
- Understand the concept of digital vortex and the impact of digitization on various industries.

MODULE 1 学以致用

1. _____(数字世界) have had a profound impact on how data and information are collected, stored, and communicated about organizations and individuals.

2. _____(数字漩涡) refers to the disruptive impact of digital technologies on traditional industries and business models.

MODULE 2 手不释卷

A. Read the following information about the digital world and business environment.

1. The Industrial Revolutions (Shown in Exhibit 7-1)

  Since the 18th century, humanity has experienced four industrial revolutions. Each industrial revolution has brought about significant technological advancements that have shaped people's lifestyles, transformed businesses, and impacted the accounting profession. At the same time, each industrial revolution has also spurred innovation in management theories, helping organizations adapt to the changing times and improve their operations.

Companies that have been able to undergo rapid transformation during these industrial revolutions, leveraging the advantages of technologies, have risen to become well-known enterprises. On the other hand, some companies have been left behind in the tide of technological change and have become part of history.

Industrial Revolution	Main Technologies/ Inventions	Impact on People's Lifestyles	Impact on Accounting Profession
1st Industrial Revolution	Water and steam power, mechanization of production	Shift from manual labor to machine-driven production, urbanization, creation of factory jobs	N/A
2nd Industrial Revolution	Electricity, mass production	Widespread availability of electric power, emergence of consumer goods, improvement in transportation and communication	Development of managerial accounting techniques to analyze costs and improve decision-making
3rd Industrial Revolution	Electronics, information technology, automation	Automation of manufacturing processes, increased use of computers and electronic devices	Adoption of computerized accounting systems, increased focus on data analysis and decision support
4th Industrial Revolution	Digital technology, artificial intelligence, big data, cloud computing, Internet of Things, etc.	Connected devices, personalized products and services, e-payment, increased reliance on digital technologies	Adoption of advanced data analytics, increased demand for strategic financial insights, emphasis on digital skills

Exhibit 7-1　The Industrial Revolutions

2. Business in the Digital World (Shown in Exhibit 7-2)

The increasing levels of digital technology in our everyday lives, commonly referred to as the digital world, have had a profound impact on how data and information are collected, stored, and communicated about organizations and individuals. In the digital world, business organizations are experiencing significant changes and dynamics that are shaping the way they operate. These changes can be categorized into several key areas.

Exhibit 7-2　Business in the Digital World

1) Lower Transportation and Communication Costs

Digital technologies have transformed the way businesses communicate and transport goods and services, leading to reduced costs. Advancements in telecommunication and transportation technologies have made it easier and more cost-effective for businesses to connect with customers, suppliers, and partners globally, enabling faster and more efficient business operations.

2) Greater Customer Expectations for Products and Services

Digitalization has empowered customers with access to information, choices, and convenience like never before. As a result, customer expectations for products and services have increased, with demands for personalized experiences, seamless interactions, and convenient access. Businesses need to adapt and meet these heightened customer expectations to stay competitive in the digital age.

3) Gains in Efficiency and Productivity

Digital technologies have the potential to streamline business processes, automate tasks, and enhance productivity, leading to increased efficiency and value creation. Automation of repetitive tasks, data-driven decision-making, and advanced analytics can enable businesses to optimize operations, reduce costs, and improve overall performance.

4) Disruption in the Labour Market

The digital world has also brought about changes in the labor market, with automation and artificial intelligence potentially displacing certain jobs while creating new ones. Businesses need to adapt to this changing labor landscape, retrain employees, and leverage digital technologies to enhance workforce productivity and agility.

5) Opportunities to Enhance Existing Products with Digital Capabilities

Digital technologies provide opportunities for businesses to enhance their existing products or services with digital capabilities. For example, adding Internet of Things (IoT) sensors to products to enable remote monitoring, incorporating artificial intelligence for personalized recommendations, or leveraging data analytics to gain insights into customer behavior can create new value propositions and competitive advantages.

6) Technologies Disrupting Industries and Supply Chains

Digital technologies have the potential to disrupt entire industries and supply chains. For example, the rise of e-commerce has disrupted traditional retail models, and digital platforms have transformed how businesses connect with customers and partners.

Businesses need to anticipate and adapt to these disruptions, or risk being left behind.

7) Increased Collaborative Innovation Between Organizations

Digital technologies have facilitated increased collaboration and innovation between organizations. Businesses can collaborate on joint projects, share data, and leverage each other's expertise through digital platforms and ecosystems. This collaborative approach to innovation can lead to faster product development, improved customer experiences, and shared resources.

3. Digital Vortex (Shown in Exhibit 7-3)

Digital Vortex refers to the disruptive impact of digital technologies on traditional industries and business models, leading to significant changes in consumer behavior, business operations, and competitive landscapes. It represents the rapid and transformative effects of digital disruption on various industries.

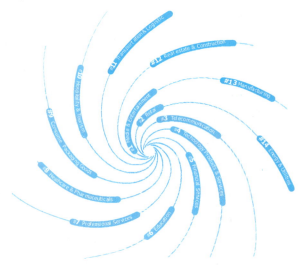

Exhibit 7-3　Digital Vortex

"Digital Vortex 2021" is authored by the Global Center for Digital Business Transformation. This report gives detailed information about the disruptive impact of digital technologies on traditional industries.

1) Media and Entertainment

Digital disruption has had a profound impact on traditional print media, social media, music, TV, and film industries. The rapid growth of streaming services has led to traditional box office revenues being surpassed by streaming revenues, further accelerating the pace of digital disruption. Many film production companies chose to release movies simultaneously online and offline, changing the traditional business model of the film industry.

2) Retail

The rapid growth of e-commerce has put significant pressure on traditional retail. E-commerce giants such as Amazon, Alibaba, Zalando, etc., have captured an increasing share of the online retail market. E-commerce has not only brought convenience to consumers in shopping, but also driven the development of e-payment and logistics industries.

3) Telecommunication

The telecommunication industry has been undergoing significant changes due to technological advancements, such as 5G, Internet of Things, and increased connectivity. The demand for high-speed Internet, mobile services, and digital communication has been growing exponentially, leading to increased competition and innovation in the telecommunication industry.

4) Technology Products & Services

The technology products and services industry has been in a constant state of change, including areas such as artificial intelligence, Internet of Things, cloud computing, big data, etc. Emerging technologies and innovations are driving changes in business models and market dynamics. Global digital transformation and digital innovation have had a profound impact on the technology products and services industry.

5) Financial Services

The financial services industry is under pressure to undergo digital transformation, including the rise of financial technology (Fintech), e-payments, blockchain, and other technology applications. Traditional financial institutions need to constantly innovate and change to cope with the challenges of the digital era. Changing consumer expectations and demands for financial services are driving changes in the financial services industry.

6) Education

The widespread adoption of digital technology has enabled more efficient allocation of educational resources. Many schools and educational institutions have adopted online teaching and distance learning models, driving the development of educational technology. Students and educators can log in from both mobile and PC devices, and access live courses or recorded lectures. Users can arrange their learning plans according to their own preferences.

7) Professional Services

The professional services industry, including consulting, legal, accounting, and other professional services, is experiencing changes driven by digital transformation. Artificial intelligence and other technologies are changing the way professional services are delivered, increasing efficiency and changing customer expectations. The need for agile and flexible solutions, digital tools, and data-driven insights is reshaping the professional services industry.

B. Learn the new words and phrases in the above passage and try to make sentences with them.

New Words

dynamics	[daɪˈnæmɪks]	n. (复数)动态
efficiency	[ɪˈfɪʃnsi]	n. 效率；效能
disruption	[dɪsˈrʌpʃn]	n. 中断；扰乱
workforce	[ˈwɜːrkfɔːrs]	n. 劳动力；员工队伍
capability	[ˌkeɪpəˈbɪlɪti]	n. 能力；才能；潜力
anticipate	[ænˈtɪsɪpeɪt]	v. 预期；预料；预测
e-commerce	[ˈiːkɒmɜːrs]	n. 电子商务
fintech	[ˈfɪntek]	n. 金融科技
reshape	[ˌriːˈʃeɪp]	v. 改变形态；重塑
telecommunication	[ˌtelɪkəˌmjuːnɪˈkeɪʃn]	n. 电信；通信；远程通信

Useful Expressions and Knowledge

1. transportation and communication costs 交通和通信成本
2. customer expectations 客户期望
3. industrial revolution 工业革命
4. emerging technologies and innovations 新兴技术和创新
5. collaborative innovation 协同创新
6. streaming services 流媒体服务
7. Internet of Things 物联网

C. Test your understanding.

Match the words listed in the following box with the effects of digital disruption on various industries listed below.

A. Media and entertainment
B. Retail
C. Telecommunication
D. Technology products & services
E. Financial services
F. Education
G. Professional services

(1) Many film production companies chose to release movies simultaneously online and offline, changing the traditional business model of the film industry. (　　)

(2) E-commerce bring convenience to consumers in online shopping, as well as put significant pressure on traditional shopping patterns. (　　)

(3) The demand for high-speed Internet, mobile services, and digital communication has been growing exponentially, leading to increased competition and innovation. (　　)

(4) Global digital transformation and digital innovation have had a profound impact on such areas as artificial intelligence, Internet of Things, cloud computing, big data, etc. (　　)

(5) Traditional financial institutions need to constantly innovate, including the rise of financial technology (Fintech), e-payments, blockchain, and other technology applications. (　　)

(6) Many schools and institutions have adopted online teaching and distance learning models. (　　)

(7) Digital technologies are changing the way consulting services are delivered, increasing efficiency and changing customer expectations. (　　)

MODULE 3 博学多才

Visit the relevant website and write down some useful information you've learnt from it in English.

https://imd.cld.bz/Digital-Vortex-2021

推荐理由：《数字漩涡报告2021》全文，介绍数字化对各行各业的影响。

LESSON 2
TECHNOLOGIES IN A DIGITAL WORLD

GOALS 学习目标

- Understand the basic concepts of key technologies, including cloud computing, big data, robotic process automation and artificial intelligence.
- Understand the impact of these key technologies on finance functions.

MODULE 1 学以致用

1. _____(云计算) is a model for enabling convenient, on-demand network access to a shared pool of configurable computing resources.

2. _____(大数据) is data that exceeds the capabilities of traditional relational methods for effective analysis due to its volume and velocity of collection.

3. _____(机器人流程自动化) is an automation technology that uses software robots or "bots" to simulate and automate routine, repetitive, and predictable tasks performed by humans in business processes.

4. _____(人工智能) is the ability of machines or computer systems to exhibit human-like intelligence and cognitive capabilities.

MODULE 2 手不释卷

A. Read the following information about technologies in a digital world.

1. Cloud Computing (Shown in Exhibit 7-4)

　　1) Basic Concepts

　　National Institute of Standards and Technology (NIST) defines cloud computing as a

Exhibit 7-4   Cloud Computing

model for enabling convenient, on-demand network access to a shared pool of configurable computing resources (including networks, servers, storage, applications, and services) that can be rapidly provisioned and released with minimal management effort or interaction with the service provider. Cloud computing is based on increasing, using, and delivering related services over the Internet, typically involving dynamically scalable and often virtualized resources.

2) Characteristics of Cloud Computing

◇ High Reliability

Cloud computing technologies primarily use redundancy for data processing services. With a large number of computer clusters, the probability of errors occurring in the system increases. However, redundancy helps to reduce the probability of errors and ensures data reliability.

◇ Service-oriented

Cloud computing is essentially a digital service that is more convenient than traditional computing services. Users can obtain corresponding services without understanding the specific mechanisms of cloud computing.

◇ High Availability

Cloud computing technologies have high availability in terms of storage and computing capabilities. Compared to traditional computing technologies, cloud computing technologies offer higher service quality and intelligent node detection, which does not impact the system while troubleshooting.

◇ Cost-effectiveness

The construction cost of a cloud computing platform is much lower than that of a supercomputer, while its performance is comparable. This results in significant cost savings in development.

◇ Service Diversity

Users have greater flexibility in service selection, with different levels of services available at different costs.

◇ Programming Convenience

Cloud computing platforms provide users with good programming models, allowing users to create programs according to their needs, which provides great convenience and saves development resources.

3) Classification of Cloud Computing (Shown in Exhibit 7-5)

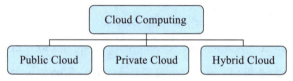

Exhibit 7-5　Classification of Cloud Computing

Cloud computing can be classified from the perspective of service mode into public cloud, private cloud, and hybrid cloud.

Public cloud is considered to be the main form of cloud computing. It typically refers to the cloud services provided by third-party providers that are accessible to authorized users over the Internet. Public cloud is known for its low cost and core attribute of shared service resources. Currently, public cloud holds a significant market share.

Private cloud is a form of cloud computing where organizations build and use cloud within their own infrastructure. Private cloud is deployed on the existing infrastructure of an enterprise and is designed for internal users. This allows organizations to have effective control over data security and service quality. Private cloud can be deployed within the firewall of an enterprise's data center and its core attribute is dedicated resources. Private cloud can be built on the enterprise's local area network, integrated with internal systems such as monitoring systems and asset management systems, which facilitates better integration and management of internal systems. Although private cloud offers higher data security compared to public cloud, it also comes with higher maintenance costs (especially for small and medium-sized enterprises), so typically only large enterprises adopt this type of cloud platform. Another scenario is when an enterprise, especially an Internet company, has already developed a mature and sufficient infrastructure and operations team, building its own private cloud may be more cost-effective than purchasing public cloud services.

Hybrid cloud combines the advantages and disadvantages of both public cloud and private cloud, and has rapidly gained popularity in recent years. Hybrid cloud considers both data security and resource sharing, and provides personalized solutions to achieve cost savings, which makes it increasingly favored by enterprises.

4) Application of Cloud Computing

Financial Cloud is an application scenario of cloud computing that leverages the advantages of cloud computing to deploy financial software in the cloud and access and use it through the Internet. With Financial Cloud, enterprises do not need to install and maintain financial management software locally, but can directly access financial management applications in the cloud through the Internet, achieving flexibility, scalability, and cost-effectiveness in financial management.

Combining the advantages of financial software and cloud computing technology, Financial Cloud provides a range of financial management tools and functions, such as financial report generation, accounting processing, budget management, cost control, financial analysis, etc., to help enterprises achieve automation and centralization in financial management. It can also integrate with relevant national systems through interfaces to achieve automatic tax calculation, automatic tax payment, IT auditing, and other functions, providing enterprises with a flexible, efficient, and secure way of financial management.

2. Big Data (Shown in Exhibit 7-6)

Exhibit 7-6 Big Data

1) Basic Concepts

The definition of big data by the National Institute of Standards and Technology (NIST) is data that exceeds the capabilities of traditional relational methods for effective analysis due to its volume, velocity of collection, or limitations in data representation, and requires significant horizontal scaling techniques for efficient processing.

2) Characteristics of Big Data (Shown in Exhibit 7-7)

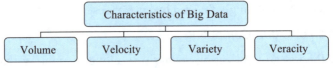

Exhibit 7-7　Characteristics of Big Data

Big data is characterized by its volume, velocity, variety, and veracity, often referred to as the "4Vs" of big data.

◆ Volume

Big data refers to massive amounts of data that cannot be easily managed, processed, and analyzed using traditional methods. This data can come from various sources, such as social media, sensors, devices, websites, and other digital platforms.

◆ Velocity

Big data is generated and collected at a high speed and in real-time or near real-time. This requires efficient and fast processing methods to capture, store, and analyze the data in a timely manner to extract insights and value from it.

◆ Variety

Big data encompasses data in various formats, structures, and types, including structured data (such as databases and spreadsheets), unstructured data (such as text, images, videos, and social media posts), and semi-structured data (such as emails and log files). This diversity of data types requires advanced techniques for data integration, analysis, and visualization.

◆ Veracity

Big data may contain inconsistencies, inaccuracies, and uncertainties due to its size, variety, and speed of generation. Ensuring the quality, reliability, and integrity of big data can be challenging, and data validation, cleaning, and governance are crucial for obtaining accurate insights and making informed decisions.

3) Application of Big Data

Accounting big data refers to the use of large-scale and complex data sets in the field of accounting to gain insights, make informed financial decisions, and improve financial performance. It involves the application of advanced data analytics techniques to process, analyze, and interpret massive amounts of data generated from various sources, such as financial transactions, market data, and economic indicators.

Big data technology provides accountants with access to vast amounts of data that can be used to uncover patterns, trends, and insights that may not be apparent through traditional accounting methods. This enables accountants to make more informed and data-driven financial decisions.

Accountants provide the necessary domain knowledge and expertise to interpret and analyze the financial implications of the data. Accountants can apply their accounting principles, standards, and financial analysis skills to interpret the data and provide meaningful insights to support financial reporting, risk management, and strategic planning.

3. Robotic Process Automation (Shown in Exhibit 7-8)

Exhibit 7-8　Robotic Process Automation

1) Basic Concepts

Robotic Process Automation (RPA) is an automation technology that uses software robots or "bots" to simulate and automate routine, repetitive, and predictable tasks performed by humans in business processes. RPA technology integrates with existing applications, systems, and business processes by mimicking and automating user interface operations, without making changes to the underlying systems or processes.

2) Characteristics of RPA

◇ Automation of Rule-based Tasks

RPA is primarily used for automating tasks that are rule-based, repetitive, and predictable, such as data input, data processing, file handling, report generation, etc. By automating these tasks, RPA reduces human errors and improves work efficiency.

◆ Simulation of User Interface Operations

RPA technology integrates with existing systems and applications by simulating user interface operations, such as keyboard inputs, mouse clicks, screen captures, etc. This allows RPA to automate business processes without making changes to the existing systems and applications.

◆ Configurability and Flexibility

RPA technology is highly configurable and flexible, allowing for quick configuration and adjustments based on business requirements and process changes. This enables RPA to adapt to different business environments and process requirements.

◆ Rapid Implementation and Low Cost

Compared to traditional software development and system integration, RPA can be implemented more quickly and at lower costs. RPA technology is typically configured and developed using graphical interfaces, without complex coding and system modifications, reducing implementation and maintenance costs.

◆ Support for Multi-system Integration

RPA technology can integrate with various types of systems and applications, including traditional Customer Relationship Management (CRM) systems, Enterprise Resource Planning (ERP) systems, databases, web applications, etc. This allows RPA to automate business processes in multi-system environments and facilitate data interchange and transfer.

◆ Scalability and Collaboration

RPA technology can be scalable, supporting multiple robots to execute tasks concurrently, and thereby improving processing capacity and efficiency. Additionally, RPA can be combined with other automation technologies such as Artificial Intelligence (AI) and Machine Learning (ML) to achieve more complex automation processes and tasks.

3) Application of RPA

RPA audit robot is an automated tool based on RPA technology used to perform audit tasks and processes. RPA audit robots automate a range of audit activities, including data sampling, data reconciliation, anomaly detection, and audit procedure execution, by simulating and executing human-like operations. This helps improve audit efficiency, reduce error rates, and enhance the accuracy and reliability of audits.

RPA audit robots are typically integrated into existing audit systems and processes, connecting with existing software applications and databases to automate the processing of large volumes of audit data and tasks, reducing the need for manual processing and human intervention. RPA audit robots can execute complex audit procedures based on predefined rules and logic, and generate audit reports and compliance reports.

It's important to note that RPA audit robots do not replace audit professionals, but rather assist auditors in performing repetitive and tedious audit tasks, allowing auditors to focus on higher-level audit work such as data analysis, risk assessment, and audit conclusion formulation.

4. Artificial Intelligence (Shown in Exhibit 7-9)

Exhibit 7-9　Artificial Intelligence

1) Basic Concepts

Artificial Intelligence (AI) refers to the ability of machines or computer systems to exhibit human-like intelligence and cognitive capabilities, including learning, reasoning, problem-solving, and decision-making. AI involves the development of algorithms and models that allow machines to process and analyze data, learn from experience, adapt to new information, and perform tasks that typically require human intelligence.

2) Subsets of AI

✧ Machine Learning

This subset of AI involves the development of algorithms and models that enable machines to learn from data without being explicitly programmed. Machine learning is used in applications such as image recognition, natural language processing, and recommendation systems.

◆ Computer Vision

It focuses on enabling machines to interpret and understand visual information from the world, such as images and videos. Computer vision is used in applications such as facial recognition, object detection, and autonomous vehicles.

◆ Natural Language Processing (NLP)

This subset of AI involves enabling machines to understand, interpret, and generate human language. NLP is used in applications such as language translation, sentiment analysis, and voice assistants.

◆ Expert Systems

It involves the development of systems that mimic human expertise in a specific domain. Expert systems are used in applications such as medical diagnosis, financial planning, and legal analysis.

◆ Cognitive Computing

This subset of AI involves the development of systems that can mimic human cognitive abilities, such as perception, reasoning, and decision-making. Cognitive computing is used in applications such as virtual assistants, fraud detection, and personalized healthcare.

3) Application of AI

Intelligence accounting, also known as intelligent or smart accounting, refers to the application of artificial intelligence (AI) technologies in the field of accounting. It involves leveraging advanced technologies such as machine learning, natural language processing, data analytics, and automation to enhance the efficiency, accuracy, and decision-making capabilities of accounting processes. These tools use AI technologies to analyze financial data, evaluate different scenarios, and provide recommendations for optimizing financial performance.

AI technologies can greatly enhance the efficiency and accuracy of accounting processes, while accounting data provides the necessary input for training and improving AI algorithms. For example, Intelligence accounting employs machine learning algorithms to analyze historical financial data and make accurate predictions about future financial outcomes, such as revenue forecasts, expense projections, and cash flow management. This helps organizations in strategic planning and financial forecasting. Also, intelligence accounting provides decision support tools that assist accountants and financial managers in making informed decisions.

B. Learn the new words and phrases in the above passage and try to make sentences with them.

New Words

corresponding	[ˌkɔːriˈspɒndiŋ]	*adj.* 相应的；一致的
mechanism	[ˈmekənizəm]	*n.* 机制；机构；方法
availability	[əˌveiləˈbiliti]	*n.* 可用性；可得性
troubleshooting	[ˈtrʌbəlˌʃuːtiŋ]	*n.* 故障排除；解决问题
cost-effectiveness	[kɒst iˈfektivnəs]	*n.* 成本效益；经济性
diversity	[daiˈvɜːrsiti]	*n.* 多样性；差异性
hybrid	[ˈhaibrid]	*adj.* 混合的；杂交的
authorized	[ˈɔːθəraizd]	*adj.* 授权的；合法的
infrastructure	[ˈinfrəstrʌktjʊr]	*n.* 基础设施；基本结构
velocity	[vəˈlɒsiti]	*n.* 速度；速率
veracity	[vəˈræsiti]	*n.* 真实性；准确性
routine	[ruːˈtiːn]	*n.* 例行公事；程序
repetitive	[riˈpetitiv]	*adj.* 重复的；反复的
predictable	[priˈdiktəbl]	*adj.* 可预测的；可预计的
rule-based	[ruːl beist]	*adj.* 基于规则的
scalability	[skeiləˈbiliti]	*n.* 可扩展性；可伸缩性
intervention	[ˌintəˈvenʃn]	*n.* 干预；介入
subset	[ˈsʌbˌset]	*n.* 子集；分支
algorithm	[ˈælgəriðm]	*n.* 算法；计算方法

Useful Expressions and Knowledge

1. computing resources 计算资源
2. data redundancy 数据冗余
3. computer clusters 计算机集群
4. strategic planning 战略规划
5. simulation of user interface operations 用户界面操作模拟
6. rapid implementation 快速实施
7. support for multi-system integration 多系统集成支持
8. data reconciliation 数据对账
9. anomaly detection 异常检测
10. audit procedure execution 审计程序执行
11. cognitive capabilities 认知能力
12. machine learning 机器学习
13. computer vision 计算机视觉
14. natural language processing 自然语言处理
15. cognitive computing 认知计算

C. Test your understanding.

1. The characteristics of cloud computing technology include (   ).

    A. high reliability

    B. service-oriented

    C. high availability

    D. cost-effectiveness

2. From the perspective of service models, cloud computing can be categorized into three types: (   ).

    A. private cloud

    B. financial cloud

    C. hybrid cloud

    D. government cloud

    E. public cloud

3. The features of big data include (   ).

   A. volume

   B. velocity

   C. variety

   D. veracity

4. What are the benefits of RPA? (   )

   A. Reduce process automation costs.

   B. Replace audit professionals.

   C. Easier to expand.

   D. Improve execution speed.

5. The subsets of AI include (   ).

   A. machine learning

   B. computer vision

   C. natural language processing (NLP)

   D. cognitive computing

MODULE 3 博学多才

Visit the relevant website and write down some useful information you've learnt from it in English.

https://mp.weixin.qq.com/s/lr9TpCmUcokPK8aRwvVkkw

推荐理由：《2022年影响会计人的十大信息技术评选报告》全文，由上海国家会计学院发布，评选出了2022年影响会计人的十大信息技术。

_____

_____

_____

APPENDIX 附录

会计专业英语能力分析表

岗位群	英语运用核心技能	专业技能点	专业英语点	知识与技能在教材编写中的体现形式
岗位1 出纳 岗位2 记账会计 岗位3 会计主管 岗位4 财务分析	1) 获得会计工作	获得会计工作	① 阅读会计工作招聘广告 ② 书写会计专业求职简历 ③ 预约获得面试机会 ④ 参加面试 ⑤ 面试合格通知书的阅读，电话接听合格通知	写作 口语对话
	2) 熟悉岗位职责与法规体系	(1) 熟悉会计岗位职责	① 熟悉出纳岗位职责 ② 熟悉记账会计岗位职责 ③ 熟悉会计主管岗位职责	口语对话 模拟情景 角色扮演
		(2) 熟悉会计法规体系与职业道德	① 了解会计法规体系 ② 了解会计职业道德并合理处理相关事务	案例分析
	3) 出纳业务	(1) 办理收银业务	① 完成现金支付下的收银工作 ② 完成银行卡/信用卡支付下的收银工作 ③ 开具发票	项目训练
		(2) 办理银行业务	① 办理银行开户业务 ② 向银行存、取现金 ③ 向银行存、取支票 ④ 办理银行换汇业务 ⑤ 办理银行汇款业务 ⑥ 月末与银行对账，编写银行余额调节表	项目训练
		(3) 工资的核算与发放	① 阅读工资汇总表 ② 发放工资	项目训练 口语对话
		(4) 报销业务	① 预借差旅费 ② 报销差旅费	项目训练 模拟情景 角色扮演
	4) 会计账务处理	(1) 审核原始凭证	① 发票的审核 ② 支票的审核 ③ 专业评估机构评估报告的审核	项目训练
		(2) 编制记账凭证	编制记账凭证	
		(3) 登记日记账	① 登记现金日记账 ② 登记银行存款日记账	

(续表)

岗位群	英语运用核心技能	专业技能点	专业英语点	知识与技能在教材编写中的体现形式
岗位1 出纳 岗位2 记账会计 岗位3 会计主管 岗位4 财务分析		4) 会计账务处理	(4) 登记分类账	① 登记总分类账 ② 登记明细分类账	项目训练
		(5) 期末账项调整	期末账项调整	
		(6) 结账	① 编制结转分录 ② 期末账户的结转	
		(7) 工作底稿编制	编制工作底稿	
	5) 财务报表阅读与编制	(1) 资产负债表的阅读与编制	① 阅读资产负债表 ② 编制资产负债表	项目训练
		(2) 利润表的阅读与编制	① 阅读利润表 ② 编制利润表	
		(3) 现金流量表的阅读	阅读现金流量表	
		(4) 合并报表(有海外子公司)	阅读有海外子公司的企业合并报表	
	6) 财务报表分析	(1) 流动性分析	① 表示流动性的财务指标的计算 ② 根据已有数据评价企业的流动性	项目训练
		(2) 资产管理能力分析	① 表示资产管理能力的财务指标的计算 ② 根据已有数据评价企业的资产管理能力	
		(3) 偿债能力分析	① 表示偿债能力的财务指标的计算 ② 根据已有数据评价企业的偿债能力	
		(4) 盈利能力分析	① 表示盈利能力的财务指标的计算 ② 根据已有数据评价企业的盈利能力	
		(5) 综合财务分析	综合财务分析	
	7) 成本核算、预算与绩效评估	(1) 成本核算	编制生产成本汇总表	项目训练
		(2) 预算	① 编制项目预算表 ② 编写项目预算报告	
		(3) 绩效评估	编写绩效评估报告	

[1] 常勋. 会计专业英语[M]. 上海：立信会计出版社，2003.

[2] 葛军. 实用会计英语[M]. 北京：高等教育出版社，2006.

[3] 孟焰，孟凡利. 会计英语[M]. 北京：经济科学出版社，2000.

[4] 于久洪. 会计英语[M]. 北京：中国人民大学出版社，2005.

[5] 张志凤. 初级会计实务[M]. 北京：北京大学出版社，2008.

[6] (美)Carl S. Warren. Survey of Accounting. 影印版[M]. 北京：高等教育出版社，2005.

[7] Michael D. Lawrence, Joan S. Ryan. Essential of Accounting. 10th edition[M]. Columbus: Thomson and South-Western College Publishing, 2007.

[8] Trotman & Gibbins. Financial Accounting—An Integrated Approach. 2nd edition[M]. Sydney: Thomson Learning Publications, 2003.

[9] Anonymity. Financial Accounting (INT)[M]. Berkshire: Kaplan Publishing, 2012.

[10] Anonymity. Professional Accountant[M]. Berkshire: Kaplan Publishing, 2012.

[11] Anonymity. Advanced Financial Accounting (INT)[M]. Berkshire: Kaplan Publishing, 2012.

[12] Alam, M. S., Hossain, D. M. (2021). Management Accounting in the Era of Digitalization[J]. The Journal of Industrial Distribution & Business, 12(11), 1 - 8.